The Music of Teaching

The Music
of Teaching

LEARNING
TO TRUST
STUDENTS'
NATURAL
DEVELOPMENT

Barbara Kreader Skalinder

Hal Leonard Books
An Imprint of Hal Leonard Corporation

Published in 2016 by Hal Leonard Books
An Imprint of Hal Leonard Corporation
7777 West Bluemound Road
Milwaukee, WI 53213

Trade Book Division Editorial Offices
33 Plymouth St., Montclair, NJ 07042

Permissions can be found on page 147, which constitutes an extension of this copyright page.

Printed in the United States of America

Book design by Michael Kellner

Library of Congress Cataloging-in-Publication Data
Names: Skalinder, Barbara Kreader, author.
Title: The music of teaching : learning to trust students' natural
  development / by Barbara Kreader Skalinder.
Description: Montclair : Hal Leonard Books, 2016. | Includes bibliographical
  references.
Identifiers: LCCN 2016008385 | ISBN 9781495059988 (hardcover)
Subjects: LCSH: Music--Instruction and study. | Music teachers.
Classification: LCC MT1.S537 M87 2016 | DDC 780.71--dc23
LC record available at http://lccn.loc.gov/2016008385

ISBN: 978-1-4950-5998-8

www.halleonardbooks.com

To Don Schwartz

contents

CONTENTS

foreword

Throughout a career as an independent piano teacher, a college pedagogy professor, and a magazine editor, I have noticed that teachers spend much of their time seeking answers to difficult questions. What is good teaching? What is learning? How can we reach every student? How do we help each student grow? What role do we play in society? As the pace of change accelerates, these questions gain a sharper focus. How do *today's* students learn? How do we fit into a society that has changed dramatically in only a generation?

It would be easy, and oh so helpful, if we could create a simple recipe for effective teaching. Collect the right ingredients (a willing student, supportive parents, a good instrument, sensible music); season well (a dash of learning theory, sprinkles of effective communication, heaping portions of motivation); mix carefully (use logical, well-thought-out lesson plans and sequences); cook (develop the ear, build technique, facilitate reading) and *voilà*—musical success!

Indeed, we are fortunate to have many books and resources that help us build our list of ingredients, understand the theories behind learning and motivation, and provide plans for teaching reading, technique, and musicianship. Well-crafted books and methods lay out a plan, provide music, and show us the way forward. Valuable ideas and concepts are central to these resources.

We all learn through experience, however, that teaching isn't as easy as following a recipe or even a method book. Our main ingredient—the student—changes by the day, both individually (we watch our own students grow before our eyes) and collectively (we see larger societal and technological forces change generations profoundly). The ideas and concepts that worked ten years ago may not apply. In many cases, what worked last week may not apply either. As change inevitably marches forward, plans and prescriptions fall by the wayside.

In *The Music of Teaching*, Barbara Kreader Skalinder provides a unique resource for teachers, one that is rooted in the experience and wisdom of a teacher who has witnessed great change and navigated through it with aplomb. Drawing on success that has spanned multiple generations, she provides valuable insight into a style of teaching that has learned to adapt as needed, always serving the student.

While learning theories and styles are destined to change, this books reminds us of important teaching elements that are valid in any setting. Passion. Love. Inspiration. Honesty. These themes consistently emerge in the author's writing, as we see teaching primarily through the lens of the *people* involved: the student, the parent, and, of course, the teacher. We see the value of flexibility and adaptability. We see a teacher who is not tied to method or tradition, but whose only goal is the success of the student. Prescription and dogma are eschewed in favor of a holistic approach that is not afraid to listen to each student and to enter that student's world in search of anything that will help spark learning.

Any book about teaching is also about learning, but this book reminds us that the *teacher* can also learn from the student. In the author's studio the students are *real*, serving as guides to aid and inform her teaching. We see the importance of working in the student's natural environment, of honoring the student's natural identity and inherent humanity. We see a pragmatic approach rooted in *reality*: change will happen, and complaining about the way things used to be won't slow down that change. Instead, our time is better served by figuring out how we can work in a shifting environment and still deliver an experience that is meaningful and lasting.

Through real-life stories and a vivid parade of characters, the author covers many important issues that all teachers face on a regular basis: Evaluation. Assessment. Pacing. Competition. Motivation. Grade inflation. Failure. Parent communication. The business of running a studio. An experienced teacher will undoubtedly meet, in these pages, many recognizable students and parents—these are people we all see in our studios on a regular basis. Young teachers will read about scenarios they are certain to encounter in the not-too-distant future. Through these anecdotes, we are treated to interesting solutions and approaches, all valuable and applicable to our own students.

The author notes that one of her goals is to be "a model of someone who passionately loves children and music and who puts both first in life." This is an admirable goal, but in these pages she "walks the walk" and shows us how doing so can positively impact the lives of so many, no matter the generation, technology, or circumstance. When we are focused on what is truly important, as this book so elegantly reminds us, teaching and learning can thrive.

—PETER JUTRAS
JANUARY 26, 2016

INTRODUCTION

Teaching seems to require the sort of skills one would need to pilot a bus full of live chickens backwards, with no brakes, down a rocky road through the Andes while providing colorful and informative commentary on the scenery.

—FRANKLIN HABIT, author of
It Itches: A Stash of Knitting Cartoons. [1]

Teaching requires competence and confidence. No one would dispute this fact, and many excellent books give teachers methods to develop both these qualities. The essays in this book will focus on a third, more intangible attribute that teachers need: perception. This includes the ability to trust both the student's natural development and the learning process itself to drive those chickens down that rocky mountain road with no brakes.

Perhaps you, like me, are a teacher who works one-on-one or in small groups with overly busy children who practice an hour or two a week, if we are lucky. Most of the essays in this book will be about teaching real children in today's digital world. Yet I begin with a story about a teacher and a group of children joined in an unusual musical endeavor. I begin with this tale because it illustrates the best of what I describe in the essays.

On any given Sunday morning, you will find the youngest members of St. Luke's Episcopal choir in Evanston, Illinois, stumbling into the choir room. Some are yawning. Others are joking around. Still others are buttoning their robes and arranging the morning's hymns, psalms, Introits, and anthems into their music folders. Indeed, they do look like a gaggle of young chicks.

The choir includes boys and girls from the ages of eight to eighteen. They are solely responsible for singing the soprano part and are equal musical partners with their adult colleagues in the alto, tenor, and bass sections. Despite their involvement with this high-level musical undertaking, they are typical children with varying talents, interests, and temperaments. They join the choir by choice and not by audition.

Enter Andrew Lewis, choirmaster at St. Luke's, ready to drive the musical bus. He, too, begins gathering the morning's music, as do the adult members of the choir. When Lewis seats himself at the piano and begins the vocal warm-ups, everyone snaps to attention.

Lewis certainly possesses competence. He holds a BM in music theory from Northwestern University and an MM degree in choral and orchestral conducting from Eastman School of Music. He studied with conductors such as Robert Shaw, Stephen Cleobury, Duain Wolfe, and Dale Warland.

Typical of many independent musicians and teachers, Lewis juggles many jobs. In addition to his position at St. Luke's, he is the artistic director of Bella Voce, music director of the Elgin Master Chorale, founder and artistic director of the Janus Ensemble, and he serves on the conducting faculty at the University of Illinois at Chicago.

Lewis also radiates confidence. He knew from the time he was a child that he would make a life in music. That commitment shines through in his every action.

Yet many musicians possess similar stellar credentials and qualities. What makes Andrew Lewis an unusually gifted teacher is his ability to attune to the remarkably varied personalities and talents of the young choristers, and to create a safe environment that allows them to learn and participate at their own pace while at the same time immersing themselves in high-level music-making.

This morning young Stephen, who entered the choir three years ago as a monotone, raises his hand when Lewis asks for someone to volunteer to sing the Introit. Stephen, who now sings beautifully in tune, intones the solo tentatively. At that point, Milos, a brand-new treble, also volunteers. Although gifted with a lovely voice, he is clearly not yet ready to take on a solo role.

Some directors would sacrifice the quality of the performance and let them sing. They would want to encourage the boys—worried about hurting their self-esteem. Others would never open the audition to volunteers and would only allow the most gifted and well-trained children to sing a solo. Lewis does neither.

Because of his musical competence, Lewis finds a way for the music to be sung up to the standard it deserves. Because of his musical confidence, Lewis lets the boys take the risk. Lewis's perceptive way of handling the children kicks in. He thanks both boys for volunteering. He then asks George, an older, more experienced treble, to sing with them. Mission accomplished. George's voice blends with Stephen's, making a focused, warm tone. Milos hums softly along. This is the equivalent of driving the bus backward with no brakes down a rocky road; Lewis is good at steering.

St. Luke's model of choral singing follows the 500-year-old tradition of cathedral choirs in Britain. The thirty trebles practice together four and a half hours a week in addition to singing the one-and-a-half-hour Sunday church service. Three of those practice hours are with the adult choir. They also sing several concerts of Evensongs during the year plus Lessons and Carols at Christmas.

This summer they also plan to travel to England, where they will sing a series of concerts at two cathedrals.

How, in this age of over-scheduled children, does Lewis keep such a rigorous schedule of rehearsal and performance from being onerous for both the children and their families? He and his wife, singer and conductor Kirsten Hedegaard, have three sons, George, William, and Henrik. All three are St. Luke's choir members. Lewis understands that various outside activities not only vie for children's time, but also make them well-rounded individuals. While consistent attendance is expected, it is not mandatory. Even Lewis's own children are sometimes absent when an important baseball or soccer game arises or when a school function requires their presence.

Yet the vast majority of the time the children show up, happy to see one another and ready to sing. How does Lewis inspire young children to love what some would consider esoteric church music in this era of Taylor Swift and Miley Cyrus? He does it by modeling the life of a musician who is passionate about this choral music, who puts music first in his own life, and who works long, long hours at what he loves. While driving down the mountain, he does indeed provide colorful commentary. He makes the experience of singing in the choir at such a remarkably high level not only possible but empowering, and yes, fun.

Over the years the children cement deep friendships that cross the lines of both age and gender. Trebles attend Anokijig every summer, a four-day music camp in Wisconsin that combines morning rehearsals of the upcoming year's music with afternoons of canoeing, log rolling, swimming, archery, and general camaraderie. At bedtime the girl trebles often play a game called Taps Talk. With lights out, they engage in a dialogue of personal questions and answers. Last summer their counselor asked them what they liked about being in the St. Luke's choir; instant responses filled the cabin:

"I just love to sing!"

"What we do is amazing! The music is really, really hard, but we can do it."

"I like being with the other kids and singing together as a group."

"I like hanging out together."

The most striking attribute of the choir music program is the way a natural mentoring occurs. The children respect and support each other, because Lewis's positive regard for the children sets the tone. Four years ago, Head Chorister Sarah stood beside eight-year-old George, helping him find his place in the music, gently reminding him which way to process, turn, and bow during the long and complex service, and serving as a model of musical expertise. Twelve-year-old George now mentors young Milos. No one assigns these jobs or pairs children together. The connections happen naturally.

The adult choir members, some of whom are the parents or grandparents of a chorister, also mentor the children. They are able to commiserate when the music gets difficult and the practice hours get long. My husband and I don our robes every Thursday and Sunday alongside granddaughters Corinne and Ella and their mother, Amy. We sometimes feel as sleepy and less than willing as they do. Yet we are always buoyed up by the pleasure of making such beautiful music together.

A most touching mentorship has arisen between two trebles who share a similar physical challenge. The older boy, in a matter-of-fact yet tender way, invites the younger one to tail him, sit by him, and join him and the others in the often raucous fun between services and practices.

You will catch Andrew Lewis giving only one stern lecture, although he repeats it as needed. It goes something like this: "I am never bothered by someone making an honest mistake. It means you are participating. What I am bothered by is inattention and lethargy. Bring your energy to this inspiring music!"

This warm yet challenging learning environment allows these

young choir members, who enter barely able to follow the service or sing a phrase, to develop into confident musicians and leading members of the group. While they are learning, the older trebles and adults provide natural guidance and support with their more experienced voices and musicianship. Girls remain in the choir as trebles until they graduate from high school. Once a boy's voice changes, he can join the adult choir as either a tenor or a bass. Some boys stay through high school, and many former trebles return to sing with the choir during the holidays or when they become working adults with families of their own.

When long rehearsals lead to the ethereal sounds of the trebles' voices floating through the nave against the backdrop of the Skinner Opus 327 organ played by St. Luke's exceptional organist, Christine Kraemer, the stones in the church return the music in a cycle of sound. I am then reminded that the contract between student and teacher is sacred. If we travel together—sometimes forward, oftentimes backward, always with our brakes unlocked—at the end of our journey, each of us will find ourselves transformed by the other.

Part One

TEACHING
YESTERDAY'S
CHILD

ENTER THE PORTALS
TO PIANO TEACHING'S PAST

The Black-and-White '50s

I began taking piano lessons in 1954, a lifetime ago. Even Captain Video, a space hero popular during my childhood, could not have imagined today's digital age. The same year I began lessons, television introduced *Ding Dong School*. Miss Frances, a woman of indeterminate age in a black dress with a doily-like collar, brought a slow-moving, linear learning approach into our living rooms. Today's children would probably find her boring, but I loved her.

The visual look of the black-and-white show, shot with a single camera, included primitive, hand-lettered signs, a bookcase with a couple of emaciated plants on top of it, and a bare table where Miss Frances conducted simple art projects.

Each half-hour episode included three or four topics. The show's music, including the theme song accompanied by a Hammond organ, had a simple folk-like quality to it, and the lyrics were designed to teach children proper social skills. Miss Frances opened the show by ringing an old-fashioned school bell. She would then look into the camera, wish us a good morning, and ask, "How are you today?" When she paused so we could answer, I usually did![1] Beginning in 1968, Fred Rogers created *Mr. Roger's Neighborhood*, a version of this linear, sequential teaching method that would be unparalleled in its excellence.

In the 1950s few of us went to preschool. Our kindergarten teachers taught us our first social skills of sharing and playing together and introduced us to the world of letters and numbers. They taught primarily by talking. Lessons included memorization and recitation. Learning to write our own name was a big event.

As piano students we were content to play folk tunes and arrangements of classical music from visually cluttered black-and-white method books and to write in our seat-work-type theory books. We heard only music played at home, on television and radio, or at the occasional adult-oriented concert.

Music magazines reflected the era as well. I regularly spent time thumbing through the stack of *Etude* magazines my piano teacher kept in her waiting room, more interested in the covers than the content. I vividly remember one that featured a young girl seated at a Steinway. Dressed in a starched pink dress with puffed sleeves, she wore a huge white bow in her hair. Even then, sitting there in my wrinkled plaid skirt and scuffed saddle shoes, I thought she looked unreal and old-fashioned.

Introduced to the piano world by Philadelphia music publisher Theodore Presser in October 1883, *Etude* presented its patient readers with four wide columns of small type on every one of its seventy-six pages. Graphics consisted of black-and-white photographs of the articles' authors, both men and women, dressed in severe dark suits, glaring at readers with grim seriousness.

Etude helped bring the piano and piano lessons to the middle class. The magazine's stated purpose was "to supply technical information to teachers about piano music and methods," especially to those teachers who did not live near large cities and had "very little, if any other means of acquiring that necessary information." The magazine took this goal seriously. "Earn a Teacher's Diploma or

Bachelor's Degree in Music in Your Spare Time at Home" blared an advertisement from the University Extension Conservatory in Chicago. Another ad directed teachers to a course created by Frances E. Clark designed to prepare them to become public-school music teachers. Columns such as The Teachers' Round Table further contributed to the piano teacher's education. Wellesley College professor Clarence G. Hamilton, and later the famous pianist and pedagogue Guy Maier, answered questions about practice and parental involvement, overeating, professional courtesy, and coping with performance nervousness. Articles such as "Music Education in the Home" by Margaret Wheeler Ross and "Why Some Teachers Are to Blame for the Failure of Their Pupils" by Sidney Silber both challenged and comforted teachers out on their own.

Etude devoted many pages to the ongoing efforts to bring professional standards to music teaching. A quote from a November 1915 article by Edward Baxter Perry discusses professional issues still unresolved today: "Teachers in some states have been working to secure laws requiring every teacher to pass examinations leading to certificates entitling the teacher to teach." The author was not in favor, however, of the "adoption and advocacy of any proprietary material of any kind whatsoever in any state system or other system of standardization."

During the editorial reign of James Francis Cook (1907–1949), the *Etude* masthead included the phrase "Music Exalts Life!" To that end, every *Etude* included fifteen to twenty scores of graded piano etudes, repertoire by master composers, and contemporary works. Much of the then-current music is long forgotten, such as "Sing Me a Song of a Lad That Is Gone," set to a poem by Robert Louis Stevenson, which appeared in the December 1908 issue. The general quality of the music was high, however, and the selections demanded more pianistic and vocal skill than the typical popular songs of today. Cooke's editorial notes in the January 1930 issue asked readers to make a New Year's resolution "to investigate new Music regularly, but not be fooled by the ephemeral freak music of sensation mongers." Under the editorship of Cooke's successor, Guy McCoy, who worked with assistant editor George Rochberg, jazz and serious contemporary music made its way in *Etude's* pages after 1949.

Day-Glo Muppets and More

In 1969, the year I began my life as an independent music teacher, the teaching world was in the midst of change. The children's television show *Sesame Street*, which first aired in November of that same year, was partly responsible for this shift. *Sesame Street* broke new ground with its learning packaged in short segments punctuated with Joe Raposo's rock-style music and lyrics related to a child's own world of day-to-day activities. Each episode exploded on the screen in Day-Glo colors. The line between real and imaginary blurred as Muppet characters and humans interacted with each other. The first show included thirty segments in one hour; cartoon-like presentations alternated with those featuring live actors and life-size Muppets.

Suddenly, five-year-olds arrived at kindergarten knowing all their letters, numbers, shapes, and colors as well as the rudiments of phonics. Schools and teachers had to adjust—to move at a faster pace, to change activities more frequently, and to add visual instruction to their oral presentations. Some decried this less-linear approach, but it didn't really matter. Children had moved on.

The piano students I taught from the 1970s through the early 1990s reflected the changes around them. They came to their first lessons familiar not only with the *Sesame Street* song, but also those composed and sung by the increasing number of composers such as Raffi and Ella Jenkins, who created CDs just for children. Jazz, brought to *Sesame Street* by performers such as Dizzy Gillespie, Bobby McFerrin, and Herbie Hancock, was also becoming familiar.

Children routinely watched pop composers such as Stevie Wonder talk about and play their songs.

If music appeared in a television commercial, such as Bach's Invention in A Minor did in a Commodore 64 computer ad, every child wanted to play it. If they hadn't heard a piece before, it was a harder sell. My students began to hear music everywhere as background noise to everyday life—in malls, airports, doctor's offices, at workplaces. A 1980s Cheney cartoon captured this revolution: grocery shoppers cruise the store's aisles while, above the ceiling, a live orchestra saws away. An increasing number of my students waited for their lessons plugged into a Walkman or Discman. The experience of listening to music was becoming less social and more personal.

By the late '80s no classroom was complete without a personal computer. In 1986 I added one to my own studio, incorporating fifteen minutes of computer-based study into my students' previously half-hour lessons. Excellent theory and music history programs for computer copied the short-segment lessons introduced by *Sesame Street*. I also began using electronic keyboards, a growing phenomenon. The ability to play with orchestral sounds and to play along to pre-recorded rhythms expanded my students' tonal and rhythmic palettes.

Children in this era responded best to vividly colored method books with Muppet-like characters, shorter units, and music that included pop, rock, and jazz-like styles. *Sesame Street* and, subsequently, schools focused on teaching reading and math less by rote and more by understanding and manipulating numbers, letters, and words. Piano methods followed suit and began deconstructing the teaching of music reading. Off-staff, pre-reading came into being. Methods that stressed intervallic reading and a multi-key approach were popular.

During these years I subscribed to the magazine *Clavier*. Published by the Instrumentalist Company of Evanston, Illinois, with

Dorothy Ream Packard as its founding editor and business manager, *Clavier* guided pianists from 1950 to 2009.

Incisive interviews with keyboard artists from Arthur Rubinstein to Murray Perahia, coupled with in-depth teaching articles by the likes of Celia Mae Bryant, Louis Crowder, Lynn Freeman Olson, Maurice Hinson, and Jane Magrath, made the magazine a must-read for both performers and teachers. One column from *Etude* made its way into *Clavier*. Frances Clark continued the work of her mentor, Guy Maier, when she established her column, Questions and Answers, a new version of The Teachers' Round Table.

Clavier also covered the rapidly changing piano world, turning to the new topics of group teaching and computer and electronic keyboard technologies, and addressing such issues as the changing scene for classical music concerts and the business of teaching. In the late 1980s *Clavier* took advantage of satellite technology and joined with Baldwin Piano and Organ Company to present a pathbreaking series of three live video conferences, each one viewed by over 11,000 teachers nationwide.

"Information My Way"

When the Internet came into more common use in the late '90s, children's learning changed again. Children's television responded accordingly. Shows such as *Dora the Explorer*, begun in 2000, introduced the character Backpack, keeper of all the technological tools Dora and her friends needed to map their way through the world. Even *Sesame Street* revised its format in 2000, with the intention of broadening the scope of the show beyond the world of television and into a wide variety of interactive media. In 2001, *Sesame Street* created its first interactive website.

With more and more families gaining access to the Internet, my students relied less and less on memorization of facts; they could look up anything they wanted to know. While this meant they found it more difficult to remember the names of notes or the order of the circle of fifths, they found it easier to improvise, compose, and play many styles of music.

Even five-year-olds now came to school knowing some version of how to type, making it easier and easier to teach via computer. They could manipulate letters and numbers and could often write and read many words. In addition, they could use letters and numbers to create their own math problems and stories. Music of all styles now played continually everywhere, often mixed with videos. Video cameras and recording devices became smaller and cheaper, and children became accustomed to seeing and hearing themselves as they moved in the world. I began videotaping many of my students' lessons and projects.

My students benefited from new methods that included CD accompaniments to the pieces they studied, a focus on improvisation, and a mix of classical, jazz, and pop-style music. Electronic keyboards continued to expand my students' tonal and rhythmic ranges.

In the spring of 1990, I added another magazine to my arsenal of teaching support, *Keyboard Companion*. Established by Richard and Marjore Chronister, the magazine devoted itself to early-level piano study with articles based on the answers to questions that in-the-trenches teachers grapple with every day.

Keyboard Companion espoused Richard Chronister's reality-based approach to teaching, one well described by his successor, editor Elvina Truman Pearce, in a January 16, 1992, *Chicago Tribune* interview: "Anything that's going to last forever cannot be learned overnight. The real teacher is the one who is interested in musical literacy, not in having a kid move his fingers from one place to another. I'm sure you could teach a chimpanzee to do that. There's a big difference between an educator and a manipulator."

In 1998 *Keyboard Companion* joined the Internet revolution by establishing a magazine website and adding sound files and video clips to selected multimedia articles.

Phones, Pods, and Pads

The growth of devices such as the iPod, iPhone, and the iPad has caused a further revolution in my students' learning. They now have twenty-four-hour access to information of all types. Even two-year-olds know how to use a finger to flip through photos of themselves and to play apps on phone and pads. My students not only hear all styles of music everywhere, they are now able to hear music any time they want and to arrange it in any order they wish. YouTube allows them to view and hear musical performances from long ago; the sounds of Horowitz and Rubinstein, for example, can fill the room with the touch of a screen. Because of these videos, classical music is enjoying some resurgence. In addition, for better or worse, YouTube features numerous homemade tutorials that teach pianists how to play some of the best-loved works of the classical piano literature in a slow, key-by-key fashion.

In January 2009 *Clavier* joined with *Keyboard Companion* to become *Clavier Companion*, published by The Frances Clark Center for Keyboard Pedagogy with Peter Jutras as its editor. Jutras quickly brought the magazine into the twenty-first century, redesigning its look and making it available in a digital edition. The magazine continues to feature interviews with prominent performers and teachers as well as practical teaching articles, but has also added sections dealing with today's expanding technology and students who learn in entirely different ways than did their predecessors. One column has survived from the 1883 to the present. "Questions and Answers" is now authored by Sam Holland, who keeps alive the mentorship lineage from Guy Maier through Frances Clark to himself.

Today even preschool children would be ridiculed if they made a presentation that looked like the one *Ding Dong School's* Miss Frances made of "how sweet potatoes grow" in 1955. No school science project is complete without a video, a PowerPoint presentation with musical background, and a deep bench of facts found on the Internet rather than at the library.

My current preschool student Owen wouldn't respond well if I subjected him to a lesson that included only verbal instructions sent from the comfort of my chair. In 1969 my students came to me knowing little or nothing about the piano. As a four-year-old, Owen arrived already able to play three Beatles songs. He had picked out the tunes on his electronic keyboard after listening to his parents' recordings of the Fab Four. I can no longer say what my first teacher might have said, "Owen, you will have to wait to learn that Beatles music. Let's look at this Middle-C song about being a good boy and practicing every day." Nor can I use only the books, pencils, and paper teachers used in my day.

Instead I design lesson plans that include multimedia. Owen begins every lesson playing his Beatles favorites by ear and learning portions of new songs by rote. He then tries out the songs with different instrument sounds on his keyboard. We follow this with work away from the piano: clapping and drawing rhythmic patterns; moving those patterns around to create new rhythms; and improvising with the patterns using various Kodaly instruments. We then play iPad apps that focus on finger numbers and key names.

Owen read his first off-staff piece by organizing a series of cards, each picturing a piano key with a finger number. He then played it with an orchestrated accompaniment he was able to access at home by asking his mother to enter a publisher code number into his iPad.

Owen's mother, Rachel, who began lessons with me in the early 1970s and studied with me until her late high-school years, one day said, "Hey, what has changed? You never did all this stuff with me! We just read out of the method book page by page with an occasional piece of sheet music. I mean it worked, but seeing the way Owen is learning, I am jealous!

Part Two

TEACHING
TODAY'S
CHILD

STUDENTS IN A VIRTUAL WORLD

My eight-year-old student Adam, an intellectually, physically, and musically gifted second-year student, greets me with a smile. He stuffs his iPod and earbuds into his pocket, carefully places his iPhone on the music rack, and begins to fidget the minute I put the music in front of him. He tells me he "can't remember" how this piece goes.

Even I, a baby boomer from the dark ages, have placed my iPhone on hold and have my iPad close at hand. Yet I am aware that Adam and I are vastly different from one another in the way we learn. I use technology to enhance my linear way of learning; Adam learns by literally immersing himself in virtual spaces.

Those of us born before 1982 learned to play the piano in a one-on-one lesson with an in-charge teacher. A page-by-page walk through the black-and-white world of the John Thompson or Michael Aaron methods got us to where we were going. We trusted our teachers to choose the music and hoped they would give us a star or an "A" when they thought we played it well. The teacher, the librarian, or the *Encyclopedia Britannica* had all the answers.

Members of Generation Z[1] like Adam are used to seeking and retrieving information from the Internet on their own, which marks a striking contrast to those of us who grew up acquiring information more passively from authority figures. These children come home from school, where they interact with their textbooks or tablets, turn on the computer, open two or three windows, listen to iTunes while texting a friend, and do their homework all at the same time. Accounting for multitasking, the average American child between the ages of eight and eighteen packs nearly eleven hours of media usage into seven-and-a half hours of media contact each day. These students maintain that it is not a lack of attention but a lack of time that compels them to multitask.[2]

By college most Generation Z children will have spent

- 10,000 hours playing video games
- 20,000 hours watching television
- 10,000 hours talking on cell phones
- 5,000 hours reading
- and sent 200,000 texts and tweets[3]

They will have spent untold hours on social networks such as YouTube and Facebook. In addition, they will do this by multitasking.

I point out to Adam that he doesn't have to "remember" how the piece goes, because he can read it. As I try to get him to focus on the music, I notice that he is itching to use his iPhone. In addition, his iPod is playing faint music from his pocket. I ask him to turn it off. As he fidgets with the device, he says, "I still can't remember the names of all those low, low notes," and reaches for his iPhone to look up the answer on a note-naming app.

Earlier generations used memorization to store information in their heads. Members of Generation Z eschew rote learning, because they know they can immediately look up whatever they want or need to know. They prefer information delivered rapidly, prefer graphics to reading, random as opposed to sequential access to information, games to seat work, and are fascinated by new technology that works interactively. They find it easier to access information visually than they do aurally and enjoy a mixed-media approach to learning.[4]

In the past, if one of my second-year students had found herself unsure of note names or intervals, I would have whipped out flash cards, board games, and note spellers. Today I open my iPad to a music-reading app called *My Note Games* and place it on the music stand. Suddenly Adam is all attention. For fifteen minutes he not only identifies note names and intervals, he also plays increasingly longer and more difficult sight-reading examples. He loves the time pressure and the swirling medal that appears after each successful performance. We go back to his original piece. Adam still looks at it blankly, until I say, "If the first phrase of that piece were displayed on the iPad music game, how would you play it?" He gets every note correct on the first try.

Students in Adam's generation prefer learning sections of knowledge out of context and feel hemmed in by linear learning. Without my saying anything, Adam scans Bill Boyd's "Swing-a Ling" to see if any of the other phrases in the piece are like the first one. "I want to learn this piece as fast as possible, because I have something to show you," he says. This need for speed and the eagerness to get on to the next task are also typical of Adam's generation.[5]

I decide to capitalize on his impatience. After Adam has identified and played the three different types of phrases, I ask him if he can think of a visual way to show me how all the parts go together. He grabs a pencil and sketches a quick map of the piece using numbers to identify each phrase. I ask him to play each phrase in random order before I ask him to put the piece together as Bill Boyd composed it. Adam then suggests a different order that he thinks "might sound better." For next week, I suggest he improvise his own piece in the style of "Swing-a Ling" as well as practice the piece in its original form.

Adam gets antsy again. He is eager to show me what he has

leaned on his own over the weekend: the first section of *Arabesque*. He proudly plays it for me—slowly but with only a few missteps. "How did you learn it?" I ask. "From YouTube," he replies.

Today's youth are more assertive information seekers, and this shapes how they approach learning. They choose which teaching techniques work for them. They are less willing to absorb what is put before them and prefer to learn in an interactive environment with their peers, using an inquiry-based approach.[6]

Adam and two friends found a tutorial on YouTube that showed them how to play Bürgmuller's popular piece key by key. I attempt to find it on my iPad and watch as Adam becomes impatient with my abilities. "May I do it for you?" he asks. Younger generations often trust technology and their peers more than their teachers[7] and I don't want to go down that slippery slope. I decline his help and manage to find the clip quickly. The video is of medium quality but successfully teaches its material. I point out the "teacher's" poor hand position and suggest several fingering changes, which Adam cheerfully accepts.

Members of Generation Z have a naïve trust in the information they find on the Internet. I never fail to discuss the quality of what my students discover, much like teachers in my day taught us how to read newspapers critically. In the weeks ahead I will guide Adam toward playing *Arabesque* with a more flowing tempo, dynamic shading, and added pedal.

Now that computerized devices are mobile, the next generation of students will be able to learn in a time, place, and pace of their own. These digitally literate learners will be always connected, increasingly independent, and able to learn from teachers across the globe.[8] It is not enough that teachers be familiar with technology and accept that learning may occur in these places; we must live within these virtual environments ourselves so that we can experience the world in the same way as our students.

During the final portion of Adam's lesson, I turn to one of piano teaching's oldest series; *Dozen a Day* by Edna Mae Burnam. These are books even a Generation Z member can love! Adam turns to "Brushing Your Teeth," which features sixteenth-note, one-measure patterns. Edna Burnam was ahead of her time when it came to chunking information, and the stick-figure avatars still illustrate each technical movement perfectly.

"Hey, these are fun," Adam says. "That deep-breathing guy on the next page is really funny." Adam gathers up all his technology, loads his iPod into his bulging backpack, hops onto his skateboard with his iPhone in hand, and is off to hockey practice. I watch him text as he rides.

THE PRESSURED CHILD

As teachers of today's over-scheduled children, we would all recognize this call:

"Hi, this is Bonnie, Jason's mother. Jason won't be able to come to his lesson for the next few weeks because of [hockey, baseball, the school play, band]. We wondered if you have a different lesson time for him or if you would mind if he skipped several weeks." Of course, this other activity is scheduled in an unchangeable time slot and the lesson time they would like is 7 a.m. on Wednesday or 4:30 p.m. on Sunday.

For more years than I care to admit, I wavered between two responses to this problem: demand or understand.

Some days, Walter Mitty style, I would imagine becoming the demanding soccer coach who made one of my students so nervous about being late to practice that he continually fidgeted and looked at the clock during his piano lesson. He lived in fear of having to run a mile around the track as punishment for tardiness. What, I thought to myself, would happen if I said, "If you are late to your lesson, you will have to stay after and play all twenty Hanon exercises in all twenty-four keys."

Instead, I slipped into my second and more typical response. With much work, I changed the child's time to a non-soccer practice day and peaceful lessons resumed. Inside, though, I felt like a wimp, angry at myself for caving in.

One year I took a stand. I challenged all my students. They could choose one or both of the following options:

- Practice an hour every day for a hundred days.
- For one week, practice as many hours as you spend each week on your most time-consuming outside activity.

Out of forty-five students, six completed the first option. Three were in one family, and they were already practicing well despite the fact that their mother was going through treatment for a serious illness! At the spring recital, everyone noticed how much progress these students had made and how well they played. These parents also noticed that their child's enthusiasm for music increased as he or she became more skillful at it.

Only four students chose the second option, but I made every family compute the number of hours their child spent on their most demanding outside activity. Parents and students were amazed. For example, soccer asked for a commitment of six hours a week; swimming asked for twelve; school plays required ten hours a week for the six weeks prior to the show and an unmentionable number the week of the production. Some children spent five to seven hours a week at the computer or three or four watching television.

When I asked one child what would happen if she practiced six hours a week, her eyes widened and she said, "I would be pretty good! You would have to give me a lot more music." My point exactly. I wanted the children to realize why they are such fantastic hockey, soccer, and baseball players, and that they could be equally amazing musicians—if they just put in the time.

After this somewhat successful experiment with at least some of the students, I found myself at a crossroads. I could add more pressure to my students' lives by demanding that they:

- drop all, or at least most, other outside activities
- practice at least an hour a day six days a week
- participate in all recitals, contests, and syllabus auditions

Or I could be empathetic to their over-pressured, over-scheduled lives by understanding that they:

- want to excel in several activities
- will practice some minimal amount of time that fits their busy schedule
- will pick and choose some recitals, contests, and syllabus auditions, depending on their time and interest

Unfortunately, both options—demanding or understanding—would cause lots of students to quit. The first would ask too much and the second too little. Students would either burn out or lose interest.

After much thought, I have come up with a third option. I took to heart three quotes from psychologist Michael Thompson's outstanding book *The Pressured Child: Freeing Our Kids from Performance Overdrive and Helping Them Find Success in School and Life*:

> *Every child's trip through school belongs to him or her!*[1]
> *Every child has something to teach us about his journey.*[2]
> *Every child has a strategy, a story, and a wisdom to share.*[3]

Rather than forcing my students' development, I decided to trust it. My third option lets me relax and just be with my students. I now focus on being:

- a model of someone who passionately loves music and children and who puts both first in life
- an experienced adult, who remembers the reality of her own musical and emotional past
- a reliable witness and wise guide to the child's own journey

Be a Model

I once had a teacher who was so excited by biology that she ignited my previously low-simmering interest in the topic. She loved dissecting frogs and shared with us her fascination with the mystery of the frog's body and habitat. Her skillful teaching guided us through the rigors of surgery and of recording our journey with the frogs. Never once did she either demand or understand. She simply invited us to come along. I remember no discipline problems, no cut classes, no one failing the course. We all wanted to be there. Passion is catching!

My own childhood piano teacher, Beth Miller Harrod, completely devoted her life to music and to her students. Despite increasing arthritis, we heard her practicing several hours a day. When she wasn't practicing, she was teaching. A student of Rosina Lhevinne, Nadia Boulanger, and Robert Casadesus, her technical and interpretive skills were beyond reproach. Beginning in the late 1940s she took students to the Rocky Mountains, where they lived and studied with her for seven weeks every summer. This experience grew into Rocky Ridge Music Center, a music camp I attended from 1958 to 1963, which is still in existence today. Our teacher treated all of us as intelligent, reasonable beings and encouraged our potential and talent. Her strengths as a teacher have stayed with me for a lifetime, and I have emulated her by choosing to have a musical life much like her own.

Over the years, I have heard many moving stories from teachers who have attended my workshops. Whether I am in the United

States, Canada, Europe, Asia, Australia, or New Zealand, the experience is the same. Many hands go up when I ask if anyone became a teacher because of someone important in their lives. For almost everyone, that person was another teacher, usually their music teacher. While the stories are specific, some features remain the same in each one: someone recognized their talent, took a special interest in them, and stayed with them throughout their musical development. My teacher filled this role for hundreds of students, many of whom became well-known performers and teachers.

Once in a while, a teacher at the workshop will tell the story of a negative experience or give the absence of a model as the reason they chose music as a profession. Either a parent or a teacher thought they weren't good enough to succeed as a musician, or a parent disappeared from their lives too soon for some reason.

The outstanding documentary *Virtuosity* includes the story of the 2013 Van Cliburn Competition gold medalist, Vadym Kholodenko. His father left Ukraine when Vadym was a toddler and moved to the United States. The young pianist, who grew up not knowing him, found his father through Facebook. During the competition they were reunited.

While it certainly isn't necessary to have adversity in life to become an artist, in his book, *The Talent Code: Greatness Isn't Born. It's Grown. Here's How*, Daniel Coyle quotes the 1970s work of Martin Eisenstadt, a clinical psychologist who tracked the parental histories of 573 eminent subjects spanning Homer to John F. Kennedy.

"Within this accomplished group the parental-loss club turned out to be standing room only."[4] Among the musicians we find in the club are Bach, who lost both parents when he was nine, and Handel, who lost his father when he was eleven. Coyle posits that early knowledge that the world isn't safe, whatever experience brings that about, may lead children to the refuge of music and can unleash the energy it takes to spend the long hours necessary to become an accomplished musician.

Remember the Reality of Your Own Journey

Children need us to remember the reality of our own musical and emotional journey. This sharply focused memory can bridge the gap between being too demanding and being too understanding.

Not all of my piano study felt terrific. Despite my teacher's stellar qualities, she could be sarcastic; neglected sight reading; failed to connect theory with learning an individual piece, so memory slips were frequent; moved some students beyond their ken too soon, missing the entire intermediate repertoire; and taught only the pieces needed for competitions and recitals. Many of her other students were able to transcend these inadequacies in her teaching, but I did not make up for some of them until well past graduate school.

My mother, due to fears for me and needs of her own, continually sabotaged my practice and encouraged me to quit. In addition, I much preferred daydreaming about becoming a great pianist to putting in the hours of work it would have taken to become one.

In other words, we are all human. So often, as parents and teachers, we want to spare our children and students the pain of our own struggle. To quote Thompson again: "[We want to make] our children's lives happier, smarter, stronger, more competitive . . . we want to forget the complexity of their struggle so we can focus on simplifying our own."[5]

Yet sometimes it is our teachers' and parents' weaknesses that cause us to grow the most. I have spent a lifetime helping children sight-read well; connect theory to the pieces they are playing; memorize with ease; and learn how to practice on their own.

If we accurately remember our own lessons, we remember how much we had to struggle so we could grow. We stay comfortable when our students struggle and can lead them through any difficulty.

When I remember how many weeks during my high school years I left my teacher's studio absolutely committed to practicing three hours a day only to return the following week with three hours a week listed on my practice sheet, I am more patient with my teenage students.

Remembering how I quit piano twice during college yet have lived a life in music helps me ride out the low spots every learner encounters along the way. As Thompson says, it isn't possible to force development. If we step back and watch children rather than trying to control them, we see them reach down and find their own resilience time and again.[6]

Be a Wise Guide and a Reliable Witness

Rather than either adding to the pressure of our students' lives or asking too little of them, it is possible to be a wise guide and a reliable witness. We can ride the ups and downs of our trip together.

In his book *A Piano Teacher's Legacy*, Richard Chronister states, "Creative teaching is finding ways to help students teach themselves something they want to learn."[7] It is important to see the real children in front of us and to trust their development.

An eminent Texas piano teacher told this story about herself. As a teenager, she decided she was going to quit piano. She told her mother and her teacher of her decision. Both of them responded by saying she could quit, but only after finishing out the current year of study. Angry, the young woman went to her lessons completely unprepared and refused to play a note. Her teacher simply sat with her. She gave the young woman her complete attention, but never insisted she play. Silence filled the room. Week after week they sat together, the young woman becoming angrier and angrier and the teacher remaining calm. The mother never said a word either. She simply drove her daughter to and from the lessons. After several weeks the young woman softened. She began to play again, this time choosing to do so for her own reasons and neither to please nor to rebel against anyone else.

Thompson says, "The engine of children's learning is their own biologically driven desire to master every mystery they encounter, to understand its underlying forces. Intellectual curiosity exists in every child."[8] "We often think students have only two speeds: working hard, and not working hard. In reality, there are many ups and downs."[9]

The question becomes: Is it necessary struggle? Struggle added due to society's and parents' and teachers' outside agendas and expectations is unnecessary. The necessary struggle of learning something new born from within the child himself is something to celebrate.

We have a real, human child in front of us, and we are real, human teachers. If we trust our shared passion for music and quiet our fear of necessary struggle, we can relieve the pressure on both of us, stop vacillating between demanding and understanding, and create a growing space for the child's musical development to unfold naturally.

MUSIC'S MANY FACES

Duke Ellington once said, "There are two kinds of music. Good music, and the other kind."

Remember Francis Cooke's warning to teachers in the January 1930 issue of *Etude*: "Beware of the ephemeral freak Music of sensation mongers." For many years the serious piano teacher taught only classical music. My childhood teacher, who I studied with from 1954 to 1964, certainly fell into this category. She felt that the study of jazz and popular music weakened a child's ability to play the classical repertoire well. She wouldn't have fainted if she had found jazz or pop pieces in our music bags, but she wouldn't have spent lesson time on them either.

Times have gradually changed. Beginning in the 1970s, piano method books began to include jazz-like pieces, and teachers sometimes let students play a pop-tune arrangement as a dessert reward for mastering the meat and potatoes of their classical repertoire. For the next three decades this view of jazz and pop as being tolerated fluff persisted with many piano teachers. In the mid-'90s I astounded a group of music campers by asking them if they had brought any jazz or popular music to camp. I wanted to devote one of their class-piano sessions to its serious study. The twelve middle schoolers looked warily at me and then at one another before gingerly opening their backpacks. Every single student had scores and scores of what they had assumed was forbidden music, music they played in the practice room only when a teacher wasn't around.

Today we fail to prepare our students for the real world if we teach only one style of music, be it classical, pop, jazz, hip-hop, or rap. Frances Clark once said, "Meet the student where they are, not where you are, and not where you want them to be, but where they really are." Students long ago entered the world of pop and jazz. We teachers have long been behind.

For the past twenty years, jazz and popular music have been integral parts of my teaching. Learning the musical lexicon of these styles has transformed my teaching and my students' playing as well as their overall musicianship and ability to perform with ease. I am also more confident, when I send one of my students out to make a living in the world of music, that they will be able to support themselves.

My student Mimi, an eager twelve-year-old, recently created her own difficult arrangement of Taylor Swift's "Shake It Off." Students are often put off by the typical publisher arrangements of the latest hits. "This doesn't sound like the real song," they often complain. For example, no "easy piano" version would have kept Swift's song in its original key or asked the student to play all the notes in the highly syncopated bass part.

Her ear pods humming, Mimi had absorbed the song's every pitch and rhythm on her long walks to and from school, so we decided to learn the piece by ear. We began by playing the drum rhythm on one pitch. We then combined the bass guitar pitches with that rhythm. Most popular tunes have complex bass riffs, but they usually repeat over and over throughout the piece. Next we tackled the harmonies. This was far easier. Swift's music had the four-chord structure typical of many of today's pop tunes. We then picked out the melody, noticing the way it often outlined the harmonic makeup.

Now it was time to put it all together. This took some coordination and lots of repetition. Because Mimi had a driving desire to play this music, she was willing to spend the time it took to master the music's difficulty. In the end, her sophisticated arrangement captured every nuance of the piece. She even learned to play along with Swift's video on the iPad.

This project worked wonders for the fluency of her playing. Mimi, a highly musical child, is an excellent reader and has good technique. She tends, though, to have trouble stitching the music's parts together. Her other piece, Pachelbel's Canon, felt hesitant. The tempo varied from variation to variation, and sometimes within a variation. She didn't seem to hear this or be able to correct it, even after we had videotaped her performance. Once she mastered the Swift piece, she began to play the Canon effortlessly in a confident tempo any bride could follow.

The study of jazz improves my students' playing and musicianship even more than pop music does. It asks them to analyze a work's every chord and harmonic progression. Melodic improvisations depend on knowing the scales and arpeggios that accompany those progressions. In addition, students who master jazz rhythms find those of classical music trouble-free.

Two years ago I noticed that my students' performances of their jazz and pop pieces were more spontaneous and animated than their classical music performances. The classical pieces were correct and well played, but it was as if each student put on a strait jacket before performing them.

The following semester I began asking students to improvise in the style of their classical pieces. After all, Mozart improvised. Why can't we? Jazz taught me early on to ask students to analyze the harmonic structure of their classical pieces, and we had been doing that for some time. For example, we frequently made harmonic and rhythmic maps of every work as an aid to memory. Yet I had never asked them to improvise in this genre.

Using the drone bass found in Tat'iana Salutrinskaya's "Shepherd's Flute," my student Sam improvised a right-hand melody. He did this by identifying the highest and lowest notes of Salutrinskaya's melody and by playing either the D minor or Dorian mode between those two pitches. The piece's original phrases helped him shape two-measure phrases of his own and enabled him to create a twelve-measure improvisation.

Sam also played Gurlitt's Little Waltz in F Major. Leaving Gurlitt's harmonic progression in place, he blocked the piece's left-hand chords, which begin with a repeated I-V7-I progression before modulating to C Major and back to F. He then improvised a melody over this harmonic progression using the F major five-finger pattern and the leading tone one half-step below the tonic.

The results of this experiment in classical improvisation were immediate. Students closely investigated each piece, not because it was an assignment, but because they were curious. What was this musical material and how were they going to change it up to make their improvisation? They played with less inhibition, because they could improvise their way out of any memory lapses. Most importantly, students played this music with more expression and energy.

No matter what style of music we teach our students, it is our job to help them develop a taste for good music. Not all popular and jazz music is inspired, of course. "The One-Eyed, One-Horned Flying Purple People Eater," which I loved as a fourth grader, doesn't have the staying power of Paul McCartney's "Blackbird." Yet not all classical music radiates greatness either. It is our job to teach all styles and to guide children as they learn, like Ellington, to avoid "the other kind" and to embrace "good music."

THE TWENTY-FIRST-CENTURY STUDIO

During the first forty years of my teaching, I had three different studios of my own, the final one being a cozy house with a grand piano, first-class recording and playback equipment, and enough light and airy space to give group lessons. A separate room allowed students to work independently with interactive computer programs. Families spent lesson times doing either homework or adult work at a large table or stretched out on my couch reading or napping. A nearby kitchen was also at their disposal.

So why is my current studio a library of music in the hatchback of my 2010 Prius, a Roland MT80, an iPad, and the living rooms of my students' homes? Because times have changed and so have I.

I first began traveling to students' homes six years ago, because more and more parents were working, and more and more students had schedules that included so many after-school activities that lessons became almost impossible to schedule. A switch to seeing students on their own turf provided many benefits: they never missed a lesson; they couldn't forget their music; I could monitor each student's home-practice conditions, insisting on a reliable, tuned piano in a quiet space; siblings were free to pursue their own interests; parents were often around and could hear our lessons without being an intrusive presence; I made the acquaintance of many nice dogs. In addition, I could charge more (not one family quit or complained), which meant I could work with fewer students and enjoy downtime between lessons.

While this was all well and good, further societal changes made my decision an even better one. In the past five years the increased portability of interactive computer programs, recording, playback, and video equipment, and yes, even the printed music itself made the expense of keeping up a studio seem unnecessary.

Students in one-room schoolhouses wrote on slate tablets; now most school provide an e-tablet for every student. Children use them to read textbook material and to complete assignments. As piano teachers we cannot lag behind! If you read Leila Viss's excellent book, *The iPad Piano Studio: Keys to Unlocking the Power of Apps*, and read her ongoing column in *Clavier Companion*, you will learn everything you need to know about the iPad's all-in-one use for music teachers. In addition, many publishers are making their methods and teaching music available in electronic formats and are designing websites that will allow teachers and students to upload teaching and performing videos and to interact with each other via Skype-like and Facebook-like programs. In fact, the Internet will increasingly allow teachers to upload courses of their own, a fact that is already changing the way the publishing industry will deliver future materials.

Some teachers, both those in schools and those who are independent, now engage in reverse or "flipped learning." The student encounters new concepts via teacher-made videos, accessible on their iPhones or iPads, outside of the lesson. Students view the video as many times as they need to master the material. The teacher then uses the lesson time with the student to practice music using these concepts. Teachers can create their own teaching videos or buy them as apps. For more information about flipped learning tutorials and to keep up with the latest in apps, visit Leila Viss's website:

88pianokeys.me. In time, piano teachers, like many in other professions, may be able to teach students without leaving home!

Is this a good thing? I don't yet know, but it is happening throughout the educational community. In an article, "The Future of Higher Education," which describes the outcome of a 2012 Pew Internet Project's research, Janna Anderson and Lee Rainie write:

> *The transmission of knowledge needs no longer be tethered*
> *to a college campus. The technical affordances of cloud-based*
> *computing, digital textbooks, mobile connectivity, high-quality*
> *streaming video . . . have pushed vast amounts of knowledge*
> *to the "placeless" Web.*[1]

The authors go on to point out that the earlier sweeping changes created by the moveable-type printing press, the Industrial Revolution, the telegraph, telephone, radio, television, and computers left the basic structure of how universities produce and disseminate knowledge largely intact. One anonymous respondent to the project's survey quipped:

> *The university has not changed substantially since its founding in*
> *about 800 AD. . . . Other than adding books, electricity, and women,*
> *it is still primarily an older person "lecturing" a set of younger ones.*[2]

Yet higher education now finds itself pressed to adapt quickly to what amounts to a new way of learning. The popularity of *Coursera*, a privately held, online instructional delivery firm, which creates massively open online courses (MOOCs), cannot be disputed. *Coursera* allows unfettered, global access for millions to engage with some of the country's most prestigious universities. While these are not yet courses for credit or a viable way to deliver a degree, they show the worldwide hunger for knowledge that can be distributed beyond the increasingly expensive confines of university walls. Of course, most colleges and universities have long taught students via online courses that grant credit to those enrolled in their degree programs.

An anonymous respondent to the Pew survey said:

> *I believe we will see . . . a return to a Socratic model of single sage teaching to a self-selecting student group, but instead of the Acropolis, the site will be the Internet, and the students will be from everywhere.*[3]

At present most universities are working with a hybrid model that incorporates lectures with more peer and online learning. I am right with them. It will always be important for students to meet face-to-face with each other and with the teacher. I will never forget my seven-week summers at music camp in the Colorado Rockies, where I interacted daily with my teacher and with talented and dedicated students, who inspired me to work harder and to reach higher musical goals. On the other hand, distance learning with other teachers, access to video of the performances of world-class pianists, and online theory and music history courses would have enhanced my experience.

Bob Frankston, computing pioneer and co-developer and marketer of VisiCalc, feels that digital access to information via "clicks" will not only make institutional "bricks" less necessary, but will even further change the teaching-learning landscape: Ideally, people will learn to educate themselves with teachers acting as mentors and as guides.[4]

TEACHING TO THE STUDENT AND NOT TO THE TEST

What do we do when students forget? At the beginning of every school year, it is common to encounter students who have forgotten what we were certain they knew at the end of the last school year. Summer sometimes produces such amnesia. While this fact may not surprise us, we do wonder how much time it will take to catch up. We worry that they won't be able to pass this year's AIM level or do well in an upcoming Guild audition.

I had the honor of knowing and working with Richard Chronister, renowned pedagogue, co-founder with James Lyke of the National Conference on Piano Pedagogy, and founder of *Keyboard Companion* magazine. In his book *A Piano Teacher's Legacy*, Richard says, "Students may remember some things we do and say, but we can never be sure which ones."[1]

Richard spent several years teaching at the Philadelphia Settlement Music School in South Philadelphia. He and his colleagues from the National Keyboard Arts Associates worked with hundreds of students, who studied in groups. They researched a question that plagues every teacher: How long does it take for students to learn new material if they only hear it once a week, and how long will they remember it, when and if it does sink in?

Richard describes an experiment he and his colleagues created.

In the first week of group class, they introduced the dotted-quarter eighth-note rhythm in an exercise that asked the students to:

1. Point and count the rhythm using slow counting.
2. Point and count the rhythm using fast counting.
3. Point the rhythm without counting.
4. Play the rhythm without counting using any keys on the keyboard, using any dynamics and technique.[2]

The students did well with the exercise, but the teachers purposely did not assign the rhythm for home practice.

In class the following week, the teachers made the same presentation, making no mention of having done it the week before. Again, the students did well. When the teachers asked, "Have you ever done that before?" no one answered "yes."

The third week, the teachers repeated this exercise. When they asked if anyone had done it before, some responded with a "yes." Yet never did a child say, "We did that here last week." They thought maybe they had done it at school, or they had no idea where they had encountered it.

During the fourth week, some children interrupted the same presentation to point out that they had done it last week. No one said, "We have been doing this for weeks."

By the fifth week, the students recognized the exercise and indicated that they didn't need any help to do it. The teachers then sent the exercise home for practice.

It takes a long time for any of us to internalize new material to the point where we can use it on our own. In this fast-paced world of teaching to the test, which is going to be given on a certain date whether every student has had the time to absorb the new material or not, this fact is often ignored.

In today's world, schools throughout the nation are opened or closed, funded or not funded based on test scores and little else. The teacher assigns; the student studies; the student takes the standardized test; the district measures the scores. How often do test scores reflect students' true understanding of what teachers present?

To quote Richard again, "It is important that students learn to measure themselves." In other words, students need to be able to use what they learn with no help at all. "We are successful only to the degree that Johnny becomes his own teacher."[3]

Richard writes eloquently about the natural stages of learning, which occur at different paces for different children. He outlined three such stages.

The first stage places the new learning into the student's environment in a natural and reasonable way. It presents an idea to a child without any need for remembering or fear of forgetting. Richard uses the example of a toddler hearing a parent refer over and over to "the table." "The child absorbs this and many other similar instances (repetition) and learns. Notice, however, that we never say, 'It's on the table, table, table, table, table.' That kind of repetition dulls the senses. . . ."[4]

When a teacher exhorts the child to "Remember, this is a table," a child panics, fearing he will forget. The student's "panic has nothing to do with learning 'table.' The object of the lesson has become fear of forgetting."[5] When teachers ask, "What is this called?" Richard says, "We have driven the word from the child's mind, just as the name of an old acquaintance can be driven from your mind when you are suddenly expected to introduce him. When the child cannot immediately say 'table,' we decide he is a slow learner. But we are the slow ones."[6]

During the second stage of learning we ask children to use their knowledge. A parent might say, "Would you put this on the table?" "In the second stage of natural learning, the *teacher* always names the object."[7] At this point the child only needs to see the table among

44

a number of other objects and be able to choose it. "Nature knows that saying the name of something is not the most important aspect of learning. Nature knows that this comes to the student in due course if we prepare the environment and have a little patience."[8]

Richard felt that the final stage of learning happened when the child could answer the question, "Where is my book?" by saying, "It's on the table." Richard reminds us that "this final stage of learning is entirely up to the child. It is never forced. The child could just as easily point to the table instead of saying its name. The child enters this final stage when he or she is ready."[9]

Just because students cannot remember all aspects of what they learned last week or last year—the sight, the sound, the feel, the name of every concept—doesn't mean they fail to remember any of them. "All the stages of natural learning flow into one another with no need for one stage to come to an exact halt before proceeding to the next."[10]

Richard's words, written in 1980, were a prescient message to our test-driven educational world of today. "In a school situation, or in group piano teaching, it is not at all necessary for all children to pass from one stage to the next at the same time, unless we educators have set up some artificial barrier such as an examination, or when we say, 'There is a test on Thursday. On Thursday, you will know table ready or not.' Testing is foreign to natural education. The test is accomplished when the child moves himself into the next stage."[11]

"Too much teaching says, one time: 'This is a table.' And from then on it reminds and reminds and reminds the student that he's been told and told and told that this is a table table table. That is a bore bore bore."[12] I couldn't agree more, more, more.

I am reminded of a story the Buddhist teacher and author Jack Kornfield often tells of a little boy who was sitting at a restaurant with his parents. "The waitress took the order of the adults, then turned to the seven-year-old. "What will you have?" she asked. The boy looked around the table and timidly said, "I would like to have a hot dog." "No," the mother interrupted, "not a hot dog. Get him meat loaf with mashed potatoes and carrots." As she turned to go, the waitress asked the boy, "Do you want ketchup or mustard on your hot dog?" "Ketchup," he said, and the waitress started for the kitchen. There was a stunned silence at the table. Finally, the boy looked at his parents and said, "She thinks I'm real."[13]

Part Three

TEACHING
THE REAL
CHILD

LET THE STUDENT BE YOUR GUIDE

I once encountered a pedagogy student who forgot that a perfect lesson plan still needs to be taught to a real student. During the late '70s and early '80s, I served as a faculty member of the Northwestern Department of Preparatory and Community Music, where I acted as a mentor to undergraduate and graduate piano pedagogy candidates. Every week, my ten-year-old student Bobby bounded up the seven flights of stairs that led to my fourth-floor studio in old Willard Hall. A cheerful fellow, Bobby seemed to enjoy his lessons, played the piano well, and practiced regularly. This day he was scheduled for a lesson with a graduate student, who would be teaching her first-ever lesson to a live student.

The master-degree candidate, who was studying with the legendary Fran Larimer, knew her stuff. She had honed her half-hour lesson plan to perfection. Technique, sight-reading, theory, ear-training—all were included—as well as Bobby's first presentation of dotted quarter-eighth notes, and time to polish his already-learned pieces from last week.

The lesson began to the sound of the room's large ticking clock. While looking at her lesson plan, the teacher asked Bobby to play a five-finger pattern in D major. Looking slightly nervous, Bobby readied his hands and played a D-minor pattern, his fingers gluing one note to the other. Never looking up, the teacher said, "Good," while checking off that item on her plan. Bobby look confused.

"Now let me hear your piece from last week." Bobby thumbed through his music until he found "The Errant Knight" and played it note perfectly, but without any dynamics or phrasing. In addition, his fingering would best be described as "creative." Again, without looking at Bobby, the teacher checked off "Assigned Piece from Last Week." Eight minutes had passed. Bobby began to fidget.

"Now on to the ear-training," chirped the teacher. It was clear from Bobby's expression that he had no idea what the words "ear-training" implied. He looked relieved when the teacher plunked down a page of short musical examples in front of him. The impending task was familiar even though its name was not.

Still holding on to her lesson-plan book, the teacher played a series of notes with her left hand and asked Bobby to circle the notes that matched what he had heard. Bobby looked over at me: "I am looking at her hands. Is that okay?" he asked. The teacher interrupted his look, saying, "Just circle the notes you heard." A polite boy, Bobby, simply circled the ones he had watched her play and probably counted his blessings.

And so the lesson went. The teacher was able to cross off every activity on her sheet before the clock rang the half hour, but Bobby left feeling unseen, unheard, and unclear as to what had just happened.

Visions of my own first day of teaching flooded my memory. That sunny September afternoon I made the mistake of asking a room full of kindergartners to get up from their tables, pick up a music book, and take it back to their seats. Chaos ensued. I never got them back. "Old John Henry" went unlearned. My supervising teacher wrote on her evaluation. "Every movement from place to place must be planned and executed slowly with children this age."

No one disputes the importance of careful lesson plans, for each year, for each semester, and for each lesson. Yet even when a teacher is adept at teaching, the student can still be missing. All the energy comes from the teacher; the "robot student" merely imitates. Telling isn't teaching. The renowned pedagogue Frances Clark used to say, "Tellers belong in banks."

We need to approach every piece with the goal of teaching the student to play it to the high standard the music deserves, yet we need to create a teaching environment that allows the child to be the guide to reaching that goal. Each has his or her own learning style, personality, and learning spiral that will affect how we implement that perfect lesson plan. As the distinguished teacher Richard Chronister used to say, "The art of teaching is created out of a study of the people we teach, of how they learn, and under what circumstances they learn best."[1]

DESIRE EQUALS SUCCESS

When parents call to inquire about piano lessons, I invite them to come with their child for a free interview. Whether or not I accept this new student depends on only one requirement: excited interest. When I meet a child who is so eager to learn that she cannot keep away from the piano, I know we will get along. It's an added plus if she can sing in tune and clap back a rhythm, but desire, not talent, will make for a successful experience.

In Daniel Coyle's book *The Talent Code: Greatness Isn't Born. It's Grown. Here's How*, he cites a 1997 long-term study by Gary McPherson that analyzed the musical development of 157 randomly selected children, following the children from a few weeks before they chose their instrument through high school graduation. What predicted each child's musical success or failure? "The children's answer to a simple question . . . how long do you think you'll play your new instrument?"[1] Those children who said they wanted to "become a pianist" outpaced those who wanted to "try out the piano" or "play for fun." What McPherson learned stunned him. "Progress was determined not by any measurable aptitude or trait, but by a tiny, powerful idea the child had before even starting lessons."[2]

In addition, McPherson discovered that "with the same amount of practice, the long-term commitment group outperformed the short-term commitment group by 400 percent. The long-term commitment group, with a mere 20 minutes of weekly practice, progressed faster than the short-termers who practiced for an hour and a half. When long-term commitment combined with high levels of practice, skills skyrocketed."[3]

Fifteen years ago a local college professor called to tell me she had given herself a present for her fiftieth birthday—piano lessons. I agreed to be her teacher. Cecilia made it clear that hers was a serious desire. She wanted to become a pianist.

I quickly learned that Cecilia possesses a brilliant, incisive mind as well as discipline and determination that would make an Olympic trainee look lazy. Fortunately, she had never studied a musical instrument, so we began with a blank slate. As is common with most adults who begin study later in life, Cecilia grasped musical concepts far faster than her body could put them into play. Being a highly successful academic, this trip back to learning at a child's level frustrated her.

To make her learning more challenging, Cecilia wasn't particularly adept either aurally or physically. Because she lived a life of the mind, she was only weakly connected to her body. She often became impatient with me if I could not immediately come up with a mental solution that would bring about a faster physical result. We struggled.

Yet Cecilia practiced daily and put to use every suggestion I made (unlike most students!). Theory and musical analysis delighted her, and she was willing to practice scales and arpeggios until her mind let her body play them without continual thought. Over time she took up yoga, which brought her a better awareness of the necessary repetition her body needed to develop muscle memory of the music.

Because Cecilia is a goal-oriented person, she enjoyed the motivation of the Associated Board of the Royal Schools of Music materials and completed seven levels. She is still studying year-round for an hour each week and has played several of the easier Goldberg Variations as well as Beethoven sonatas, Brahms Intermezzi, Debussy preludes and an increasingly large portion of the classical piano literature.

How do we ignite a student's passion? Coyle suggests that such desire is often kindled from the outside: a child or an adult first hears someone important making music and says, "I could do that." Coyle uses a sports analogy to make this point. After Roger Bannister became the first person to run a mile in less than four minutes, an Australian named John Landy broke the four-minute barrier only weeks later. "Within three years no fewer than seventeen runners had matched the greatest sporting accomplishment of the twentieth century. Nothing profound had changed. . . . The seventeen runners had received a clear signal—*you can do this too*."[4]

After every recital I ask my students if they heard another student play a piece they would like to learn. Nearly everyone says "yes." One year four of my students nailed C.P.E. Bach's "Solfeggio" simply because my student Corey had played it well the year before. In every case, the music stretched the limits of their previous skills.

Desire equals success.

ONE LEARNING STYLE DOESN'T FIT ALL

At a student's first interview, I invite them to come to the piano. Once I have heard any pieces they already know or have made up, I suggest we improvise together. I find this free-form music-making helps me get to know a child's personality and probable learning style. I begin to play an eight-measure, looped accompaniment on the black keys that sounds harmonious with any black-key melody they create.

Allie was four when she first came to me for lessons. She listened to my directions: "Choose any group of two black keys on the upper part of the keyboard and use them to make up your own song." I began playing what was a slow, dreamy accompaniment. To my surprise Allie jumped off the bench and ran to the low end of the keyboard, where she began playing and singing in the rhythm of the words "pepperoni pizza." She played every black key, beginning in the low bass, skirting around my middle-bass accompaniment, and playing until the treble keys ran out. Amazed at her confidence and rhythmic energy, I quickly changed my accompaniment to match her staccato touch and boisterous mood.

What did I learn about Allie? She had technical facility. Her little fingers bounced lightly on every key, the rhythm and tone never wavering. I asked her if she had ever heard those words and that rhythm before. Her eyes brightened, "Oh, yes. My friend plays the violin." I added to my mental notes the words "excellent ear." I also learned that Allie chose her own musical mood and added her own creative ideas with confidence.

Several minutes later her older brother Daniel, then six, joined me in the same exercise. He played along to my flowing accompaniment with one note repeated over and over in a pianissimo tone. After a few phrases, I suggested he try other notes. He moved up a step where he stayed on this key until he finally gave up. He looked up at me and said, "What am I supposed to be looking at?"

What did I learn? Daniel was going to be a good reader. He would also welcome and follow specific directions and would want to "play it correctly." His sister was probably going to play fast and loose with the score and like to make up her own pieces. I was right. Allie was first and foremost an aural learner. Daniel was a visual one.

We learn through our five senses: sight, hearing, touch, taste, and smell. Some add a sixth sense, often called extrasensory perception, which allows our minds to intuit learning without our bodily senses. Music taps our visual, aural, and physical senses. Taste and smell are no help! Music also calls up our extrasensory perception in ways that allow us to interpret, compose, and improvise music. We often call this hard-to-pin-down sense "creativity."

Each child has a primary way of learning. We all recognize the student who, like Allie, learns by ear. We often underestimate the value of this talent, because it is extremely difficult to teach aural learners how to read music. These students often leave their music at home or say, "I can't remember how this piece goes," when the music is sitting right in front of them.

We welcome visual learners. They read with ease, making us feel successful as teachers. What they sometimes lack, though, is the ability to play musically or to polish a piece beyond a first-run-through-sounding performance. An often-heard refrain is: "Do I have to play this piece again this week?"

Physical learners frequently come to their lessons dressed in a sports uniform. They are generally well coordinated and play with a natural ease. When we first present a new piece, they are often looking at our hands, hoping we will demonstrate how it goes so they can copy our movements. They also ignore fingering, because they are able to play a scale using fingering such as 1-2-3-4-5-4-5-4 and still create a legato, even tone! Convincing them of more traditional fingering, or any at all, can be challenging.

Students who approach music intuitively like to change the music's notes and rhythms or to create their own pieces. What seems like an ingrained mistake is often simply the way the student prefers the music to sound. My creative student Sarah frequently prefaced her performance of the week's assigned piece with comments such as, "I didn't like the chord in the third measure, so I changed it."

Of course, children learn in a combination of ways. Allie joined her aural sense with a creative one. Daniel combined his visual sense with a physical one. Sarah connected her intuitive sense with an aural one. It is definitely our job to teach children to use all of their senses when they play, but the first step is to honor and celebrate a student's primary way of learning and to begin by teaching via this strongest sense. Once they begin to grasp a concept or a technique, we can solidify their learning by presenting the same concept or technique from all of the other senses.

Students get in trouble when one sense gets ahead of another. If their reading gets ahead of their technique or their learning by ear gets ahead of their reading, for example, they will become frustrated and might give up. A confident performance requires use of all our senses. It requires us to have read the music accurately and to have practiced it enough times to ingrain it into our muscle memory. It demands that we listen to ourselves as we play; connect the physical movements we make to the sounds we create; match our interpretation to the composer's intentions without forgetting to filter the music through our own heart; and improvise our way out of any anxious moments nerves bring our way.

When my four-year-old student Owen came to me, he could already play several Beatles songs well. Listening to his parents' recordings, he had learned them by ear. Although Owen was so eager to play the pitches he heard that he grabbed them with any available finger, he played the melodies and harmonies with amazing accuracy, style, and physical ease. How was I going to teach him to read without destroying his uncannily high expertise? "My Dog Spike" wasn't going to have the emotional and musical splash of "Hey Jude."

I let Owen continue to rely on his ear to learn songs from recordings while I gently guided him to more comfortable fingering choices. We also worked on learning to read music—away from the piano. Using a floor staff, note-reading apps and games, and Kodaly instruments, I taught Owen to read. The piano was reserved for pieces he continued to learn by ear. Once Owen could play short musical phrases using a drum or a small xylophone, and once he knew the names of all the piano keys, we started combining his reading with his piano playing. Surprisingly, he loved learning the method songs and made fast progress, although the overall process took over a year.

TEMPO AND DYNAMICS: EVERY CHILD HAS THEM

Students come to us with one tempo and one dynamic level—their own. Every week my fourteen-year-old student Eric rode his bike into my yard at breakneck speed, screeched to a halt outside my front door, and bounded into my studio. He played all his pieces fast and loud. Eleven-year-old Luke shuffled into the room with his head down. He spoke in a soft, abnormally high voice, if he spoke at all, and played with a tentative touch. Ten-year-old Charlie, the defensive lineman for his elementary school's football team, played all music at half-speed, giving every note equally heavy emphasis.

With any student, my first impulse is to match the music I assign to the student's primary way of being in the world. In fact, I believe this works. Eric loved stomping through the first section of Grieg's "March of the Dwarves." I celebrated this.

It is our job, though, to encourage our students to enlarge their emotional palettes. Eric had chosen the Grieg without paying much attention to the rippling bird-song section that lay in wait on the third page. He kept "forgetting" to practice that part, and when I coached him through the notes, it first sounded like the room was filled with screeching gulls rather than flitting goldfinch.

One day a cardinal visited the crab-apple tree outside my studio window. Before Eric raced off on his bike, I drew his attention to the bird's arcing flight. He watched in awe as it flew right by him and landed near his backpack. He then turned toward me with a sly smile. "You're showing me this so I will play that middle part of my piece with a lighter touch, aren't you?" (Of course, children see through us.) "Yes," I said. "Oh, okay. I get it." And he did.

Luke didn't like to talk at all if he could help it. At first I tried to draw him out. In time, I noticed that he answered my questions and responded to my directions with the music itself. I stopped expecting a verbal reply. Luke loved Mozart. He played it with technical clarity and beauty. The dynamic range and tonal color of the music existed, but in miniature.

One day Luke came to his lesson wearing a winter hat that featured six-inch spiky points all over it. He looked like an angry porcupine. I took this as Luke's signal to the world: "Pay attention. I am here!" I thought this was a positive message from a child who took up little space both physically and verbally. I complimented him on the hat and let him wear it throughout the lesson.

I also decided some spiky music was in order. Mozart's Rondo *Alla Turca* from his Sonata in A Major K 331 did the trick. Luke warmed to the music's frenzy and speed. He began to speak to the world through every note and phrase in a confident and forceful musical voice. Some time passed before Luke could easily chat with me before and after his lessons, and he continued to wear the spiky hat until, sometime during his last middle-school year, it disappeared. By the way, I think Mozart would have liked that hat.

Charlie didn't display a particular talent for playing the piano and he knew it. Nevertheless, he came to each lesson with good will and an eager attitude. "I'll give it a try," he would say. I liked this boy. At ten Charlie was already taller than I was. He had obvious athletic prowess, which translated to a physical ease at the piano. Musical concepts, such as eighth notes and staccato, befuddled him, however. The more football analogies I could use, the better he understood what I was trying to teach him, but no matter how I presented or modeled a piece, he played it in a slow, plodding style.

One afternoon we turned the method-book page to an arrangement of Vivaldi's "Spring." "Hey, I've heard this one!" he said. "Doesn't it usually have some violins or something with it?" I ran to my stereo and played the original. (YouTube hadn't been invented!) After listening to the music, I asked Charlie to read the music phrase by phrase rather than note by note. (Yes, I had tried this before.) This time he got it, and I even had the pleasure of hearing him say, "I better work on this so I can play it faster." And, yes, he played the eighth notes and staccato perfectly.

While it wouldn't be wise to assign only familiar pieces, they often help a student move past a blind spot. Charlie reverted to playing quarter instead of eighth notes when he began his next piece, but I referred back to "Spring," and he eventually grasped the concept. His tempo also returned to slow and slower, but I was able to coax him into a faster one, because he now knew he could do it.

SOME STRUGGLE IS NOT
ONLY NECESSARY, IT IS VALUABLE

As piano teachers we think our most important job is to teach children how to play specific pieces up to the standard the music demands. One of my potential students once said, "I already know how to play the piano." (She plunked down a few keys.) "I just need you to teach me a few songs."

Pedagogy programs do a great job of instructing budding teachers how to teach "a few songs":

> *Give children a model for the way the music is supposed to sound with your own performance, other students' performances, or recordings.*

Rigorous hours of perfecting our own pianistic skills and refining our own musical tastes give us this necessary expertise. As one of my preschool students once said, "You mean you can play the piano, too?"

> *Give students the musical and technical guidance to help them connect the movements they make to the sounds they create.*

Pedagogy programs spend the most time teaching this second step. It is an important one that requires long hours of studying piano methods; MTNA, Guild, and Federation theory and performance syllabi; the Associated Board of the Royal Schools of Music publications; Kodaly, Orff, Suzuki, Kindermusik, Music Together programs, and so on.

No one would discount the importance of these two skills. Yet as difficult as they are to develop, they are the easier aspects of teaching! The vital teaching skill we most need is the ability to choose music that allows our students to struggle just the right amount and the ability to guide them through this effort.

Some struggle is not only necessary, it is valuable! The fourth chapter of Daniel Coyle's book *The Talent Code* begins with a quotation from Samuel Beckett: "Try again. Fail again. Fail better."[1] Coyle's book describes what he calls "deep practice." Any pianist would recognize its attributes, which include slowing down, whole-parts practice or "chunking," and attentive repetition aimed at specific goals designed to build baby steps into leaps. What isn't well known is that these repetitions work because they build myelin—a substance made up of protein and fatty substance that wraps itself around our nerve fibers and acts as an insulating layer, or sheath. The purpose of the myelin sheath is to allow electrical impulses to transmit quickly and effectively along the nerve cells when we perform any action, whether we are riding a bike, batting a ball, or playing the piano.

Coyle explains: "Struggle is not optional—it's neurologically required: in order to get your skill circuit to fire optimally, you must by definition fire the circuit sub-optimally; you must make mistakes and pay attention to those mistakes; you must slow teach your circuit. You must also keep firing that circuit—i.e., practicing—in order to keep myelin functioning properly . . . practice makes myelin, and myelin makes perfect."[2]

The thirty-year work of psychologist Anders Ericsson, documented in the *Cambridge Handbook of Expertise and Expert Performance*, discovered that "every expert in every field is the result of around ten thousand hours of committed practice . . . 'deliberate practice' . . . working on technique, seeking constant critical feedback, and focusing ruthlessly on shoring up weaknesses."[3]

As Coyle puts it: "deep practice x 10,000 hours = world-class skill."[4]

While some struggle is necessary, it needs to be carefully calibrated. Too much struggle is harmful. Too little is uninspiring. In his book *Flow: The Psychology of Optimal Experience*, Mihaly Csikszentmihalyi says, "Every flow activity, whether it involved competition, chance, or any other dimension of experience, had this in common: It provided a sense of discovery, a creative feeling of transporting the person into a new reality. It pushed the person to higher levels of performance, and led to previously undreamed-of states of consciousness. In short, it transformed the self by making it more complex. In this growth of the self lies the key to flow activities."[5]

Struggle must be in areas between boredom and anxiety. Students enjoy first lessons because they have no skills and the first skills are the easiest to achieve. But they will fall into boredom if the skills do not accelerate fast enough and will experience anxiety if they accelerate too fast. It is the teacher's job to add skills at just the right pace for each child. This is no easy job!

Learning that comes with challenge is stored more effectively and more durably in the brain than learning that comes easily. How often have you witnessed a moment like this one? My student Daniel worked hours and hours on the demanding coda of the Chopin Ballade in F Minor. At the recital he played the coda with great success and up to the standard of the rest of the piece. Two years later, he chose to play the Ballade for his college audition. When he returned to it, guess which section he could still play best—the coda. Daniel came to his lesson completely confused by this turn of events. "I can't even remember how the opening goes," he lamented. "I feel like I am learning it for the first time. But the coda—I can still play it with my eyes closed!"

TEACHING STUDENTS HOW TO WORK ON THEIR OWN

Most of today's children's activities, such as schoolwork, soccer, or acting, are learned in groups. Whether we teach one-on-one or in groups, learning to play an instrument requires long hours of solitary practice. It requires the same tedious repetition and trial and error as it does to learn to play basketball, but piano students rarely have a coach nearby.

We are some of the only teachers who train students how to work on their own. Group cooperation and learning, while important, won't fully prepare children for work life in the current digital age. With so many companies now allowing their employees to work from home, the development of solitary discipline is more important than ever.

Jessica Lahey in her book *The Gift of Failure: How the Best Parents Learn to Let Go So Their Children Can Succeed*, points out: "The ability to attend to a task and stick to long-term goals is the greatest predictor of success, greater than academic achievement, extracurricular involvement, test scores and IQ."[1]

For many years I directed the Junior Sessions at Rocky Ridge Music Center in Estes Park, Colorado. Before I became the director, I served as students' practice partner. The camp's string and wind players could set up their music stands anywhere throughout the aspen- and fir-tree-lined campus. Pianists practiced in cabins sprinkled all over the mountainside. Everyone had assigned practice times and all were expected to practice three hours a day.

On the first day of camp, my colleague Jim McWhorter, gave the following instructions to his cello students:

"Just for today I want you to do the following. Lug your cello out of your cabin, find a suitable rock or tree, and set up shop. Assemble your music stand and organize your music; secure your cello into the ground; rosin your bow; tune your cello. Then reverse the process and put everything away. Whatever you do, don't practice!"

The students looked confused, but Jim would accept no questions. "Just do as I say."

The next day Jim again gathered his students. "How did it go yesterday?" he would ask.

Invariably several students would say, "Well, once I had everything out, I went ahead and practiced."

Jim would feign mock anger at their disobedience, but would then ask the students why he had given them such an unusual assignment. At least one smart fellow would usually get it.

"The most difficult part of practice is breaking away from what you are doing and getting set up."

How true.

I watched Rocky Ridge campers practice for four summers. I did no teaching. I simply sat next to them and listened attentively. I assured them I wasn't there to police them or to make certain they stayed glued to the bench during their assigned time. I didn't promise the outside motivation of stickers, pizza parties, or awards for time spent. I had long ago learned that practice hours filled don't necessarily equal practice well done.

Instead, I was interested in enjoying their progress and the music itself. I was there to help them streamline and accelerate their learning. Whenever a student had a question or needed help, I gave it, but in a way that gave them practice hints rather than taught them some new concept or interpretation. For example, I would play one hand while they were learning the other so they could experience the full sound of a passage. I might also help them make a map of the piece or help them block accompaniment patterns to make learning easier.

The most important work I did as a practice partner was simply to sit with the students. I let them know that I had practiced in these same cabins as a teenager. I revealed that I often played the parts I already knew, skipped difficult sections, took long breaks to sit beside the brook, and generally frittered away my time. I told them that once my teacher sent me out of my lesson, because I kept failing to learn a tricky transition in a Mozart Concerto. Students were comforted by this.

I also told them that I had since learned how to stick to the job at hand. I had learned to sit with myself, to ignore distractions, and to find ways to keep myself engaged with learning the music. I did this by replacing irritation and frustration with curiosity. Instead of playing a piece or a section of a piece over and over without thinking, hoping it would magically work this time, I now asked myself questions. I encouraged them to do the same: "Why did I play that note and not the correct one?" "Why am I rushing in this passage?" "Why can't I navigate this technical difficulty?" "How can I better match the physical movement I am making to the sound I am trying to create?" If we treat mistakes as opportunities to observe and evaluate what's going on and make this a method of practice, it will not only make practice more interesting, it will pay off in performance. Together the students and I often found surprising answers to our questions. Time passed quickly.

Because I had the luxury of sitting with the same children every day for four weeks and sometimes for several summers, I could watch them internalize this ability to view each musical and technical difficulty as a problem to be solved rather than a seemingly permanent stumbling block or a frustration to be endured. Over time they replaced my presence with the ability to be present with themselves. Well, sometimes they needed a surrogate. One summer my long-time student Zoe came running up the path to her practice cabin, "Hey, now I can practice at home for up to two hours at time, because I have a new practice partner. I replaced you with my dog, Gertie!"

LISTEN UP!

My experience as the camp practice partner led me to a new way of responding to my own students at home when they spoke the dreaded words "I didn't have any time to practice this week." In the old days I would become annoyed, grab their assignment book, and say, "Well, we will just practice together then." The child would cringe as I went into overdrive, ramping up my voice and hovering over the student like a dark shadow. My student, turned into a timid robot, would merely imitate whatever I did. Neither one of us learned anything. We were both unhappy.

No more. I view this seemingly negative situation as an opportunity to watch my students practice. Often this is the best way to judge whether I am doing a good job of communicating, whether I have hit the sweet spot of difficulty, whether I have given a clear assignment.

I direct my students to practice as if they were alone at home. I tell them I will simply watch without talking. (This is extremely difficult for us know-it-all teachers to do!) If the student has a question or needs help, it is up to her to ask me to join in. Often what I learn surprises me.

One afternoon Sophie, a talented ten-year-old, greeted me with the dreaded words. She had been making stellar progress and was one of my best students, but in the past two months her interest and practice had been waning. She began to practice her new four-page, early intermediate piece. For the first fifteen minutes I watched as Sophie accurately read the A section, checked and corrected a few fingerings, and worked on shaping each phrase musically. I was impressed. As she turned to the third page and began the B section, she dropped her hands to her sides and let out a huge sigh.

Sophie turned to me and said, "I am not doing well anymore." Rather than quickly reassuring her that she was, which was my true opinion, I said, "Why do you think that?"

"Well, she replied, "I used to have four new pieces a week and now I have only two."

"Your pieces are longer now."

"I know," she said. "That's the problem. I get tired of practicing only one piece over and over, even if I like it."

"How do you think we could change your assignment so it will be more interesting?"

Sophie's eyes brightened. "I would prefer to play only parts of four pieces each week. It would take me longer to learn each one, but at the end of the year I would know the same number of pieces. I would be happier if we could mix it up. I like variety!"

While I had chosen pieces that were the right difficulty—neither too easy, nor too hard—and while Sophie liked the music, I had chosen too few pieces and had not realized her need for variety. I could only have discovered this fact by watching and listening instead of talking and encouraging. We changed up the assignment as Sophie suggested. This solved her lagging interest.

My student Mark taught me to stop talking and to listen in a different way. For three happy years I taught Mark's brother, Michael. Teaching Michael felt easy. Being around Michael's younger brother, Mark, who was still too young for lessons, felt difficult. Despite parents with outstanding skills, Mark ran around the room during recitals and lessons, talked out loud at inappropriate times, and usually had to be ushered out. His unusually rigid muscles, strained, high-pitched voice, and seemingly uncontrollable energy signaled trouble. When Mark turned eight, his parents announced he wanted to begin piano lessons. I was wary, but he seemed excited and eager, and so we began.

The going was as rough as I feared it would be. Mark was highly intelligent. He learned to read music with amazing speed, but he had great difficulty getting his tightly-wired muscles to respond to his wishes. It took several weeks for him to master the simplest of pieces. While Mark was a likable fellow, who did have the ability to concentrate on the task at hand, as the weeks wore on I began to dread his lessons. No student before him had so depleted my arsenal of ideas for overcoming technical obstacles. One afternoon Mark spent nearly twenty minutes trying to play a sixteen-measure, primer-level piece. We clapped, tapped, sang, hopped, analyzed, and wrote out the more difficult aspects of the music. We even took two breaks for drinks of water—more for me than for him, I admit. Finally, I had no more ideas. None. My patience exhausted, I simply stood beside Mark in silence, realizing I was close to tears.

Fortunately, I had the wisdom to step back and look at Mark. To my amazement he appeared unfazed by this failure. His face wore no mark of the strain I was feeling. His fingers were still poised over the piano. After a few more moments of silence, he turned to me, and in an eager voice, full of trust, said, "Well, those ideas didn't work. What should we try now?"

In that moment I realized that this impossibly slow, frustrating, start-and-stop way of learning, which had exhausted my patience and brought me to a mental full stop, was normal for him. I stood there in awe of his perseverance, his good nature. I realized I knew far less than he did about meeting difficulty head-on, about trying again and again, about facing the fact that, despite all effort, you could not master a skill.

I found myself saying, "Mark, what do you do at school when you are having difficulty learning something?" He thought for a moment, and then a few more, and finally replied, "Well, I usually stand up and shake out my arms and legs." After more reflection, he went on. "My teacher doesn't like it when I do that, though. She tells me to sit down." Smiling shyly, he added, "If I could, I would also sing whatever I wanted."

This surprising revelation made sense to me. While we had been engaging in large-muscle movement and singing in an attempt to learn the piece, it all required the structure of certain rhythms and pitches. Mark intuitively knew he needed to relax his rigid muscles in a freeing way.

"Well," I said, "we're not in a classroom where your movements would bother anyone. Let's try your idea." Mark gave me a huge smile, stood up, and shook himself out in a little dance. He ran around the room, singing an unmetered, stray-pitched song at the same time. We delighted in its raucous energy. Then he sat down, and we began again to master those pesky sixteen measures.

Did Mark's idea make it easier for him to learn the piece? Absolutely. In the next ten minutes, he was playing the music with more fluency and better rhythmic precision. Did his idea solve his problems and make his learning easy? No. Mark continued to struggle. A big change did occur, though. Mark and I both looked forward to his lessons. When one or the other of us reached the end of our rope, Mark would do one of his little dances. We would laugh and enjoy the moment and begin again.

After two years Mark stopped piano lessons. Despite hard work, he had only reached the beginning of Level II. Soccer seemed a better fit for his need to "shake out" his arms and legs.

PRAISE FOR NOTHING
MEANS NOTHING

In an era of hovering helicopter parents, who feel it is their highest calling to boost their child's self-esteem, a call to honest appraisal of a child's efforts sounds like heresy. In elementary school my granddaughter played soccer in a league where the coaches and parents refused to keep score, because they wanted the children "to feel good about themselves." One afternoon my husband made the mistake of cheering on Corinne's team as it made a goal. Within earshot of our granddaughter, the coach took my husband aside and said, "Remember, we don't keep score," to which Corinne replied, "It's six to two and the Lemon Drops are ahead!"

Parents, teachers, and coaches who continually praise children do so with the best of intentions. Many of them grew up in an educational atmosphere of harsh criticism and competition that killed not only creative expression but also a child's spirit. The psychologist Michael Thompson, in his book *The Pressured Child*, writes: "We can't bear to see our children suffer. If we had it in our power to protect them from disappointments, the unhappiness, or the true misery we experienced as children or saw around us, we would do so."[1]

Thompson goes on to say, "Adults make the mistake of thinking it is possible for children to have high esteem all the time. They demand that their children's caretakers work to maintain his high esteem at high levels at all times. This cannot be done. It is just not easy to feel powerful when you are a child. How can [they] . . . when they are short, have no independent source of income, no car, and no control over their own daily schedules? How would you feel? Small indeed, and powerless."[2]

Exclamations such as, "Everybody wins!" or signs like the one posted outside our neighborhood school—*Lincolnwood: Where Every Student Is a Superstar*—delude only adults, not children. Not every child is going to be a star, and why is being a star so important anyway? If everyone wins, why are we playing the game in the first place?

Many years ago I taught a student, Rita, who inadvertently questioned the wisdom of one of my deeply ingrained teaching techniques: positive comments first. After hearing a particularly bad performance of the week's new piece, all I could think to praise was Rita's effort to keep her heel on the floor while she pedaled. With utmost respect but obvious impatience, she said, "Oh, Mrs. Kreader, skip the praise. That performance was a mess. Just help me fix it." In that moment Rita taught me that praise for nothing means nothing.

Outside praise has an inferred expectation and puts pressure on a child. Children who are told they are talented rather than praised for their hard work are more likely to avoid increasingly difficult projects. As Jessica Lahey points out in her book *The Gift of Failure*, they sacrifice curiosity and love of learning for achievement.[3] It is far better to reward children's efforts than to tell them how smart they are.

Lahey goes on to remind us that if a child who tries something challenging or new fails, "That failure will be hard evidence that she's not as smart as everyone keeps telling her she is. Better to be safe. Is that what we want? Kids who get straight A's but hate learning? Kids who achieve academically but are too afraid to take leaps into the unknown?"[4]

Children also need to learn that sometimes even effort is not enough. Is everyone's performance of *Für Elise* equally good because they made a great effort? Think of the number of times you have taught *Für Elise*. You are the same teacher, one who has full grasp of the earlier-mentioned steps one and two: modeling the performance and guiding the students as they learn the mechanical and musical aspects of the piece. For example, my students are always amazed that I can call out a correct finger number in any passage of this war horse from across the room!

Yet how many of your students have played *Für Elise* as Beethoven would have wanted Elise to hear it? In forty-six years of teaching I have had three students play it exquisitely. I have had hundreds play it well and many who were only able to plough their way through the first section. Some students learned the piece in two or three weeks, most spent two or three months. One studied it for a year!

My friend Robert Zabel, a professor emeritus of education at Kansas State University, remembers the day one of his students came to him complaining of her B grade.

"I attended every class," she told him, "and I handed in all of my assignments on time. Why did I get a B and not an A?"

"Because you did B-level work," he replied.

She didn't get it.

Alfred Posamentier, dean of the School of Education at City College of New York (CUNY) once wrote to the *New York Times*: "Students from the earliest grades are encouraged to work hard and told that the rewards will follow. Students must realize that a grade is earned for achievement and not for the effort expended."

In the same issue John Mahoney of Woodbury, Connecticut, commented, "It should hardly be surprising that this generation of college students equates effort with guaranteed success. After all, from the time they first compete as youngsters, be it in T-ball or at birthday party games, all participants are rewarded with a trophy, medal, or prize for merely showing up and taking part regardless of their ability or talent."

As adults we often forget that the word "compete" comes from the Latin *competere*, which means "to seek together." Competition itself isn't a bad thing. Children who seek to build their skills in competition with others who are more skilled than they are do better than those who learn in a vacuum. Only then do children learn that effort and result don't always match, that sometimes their best attempts fail and their less-than-best succeed.

We do have to ask ourselves, though: Is this a good competition? As a student and as a judge, I have experienced many piano contests. Frequently the child is released into a cavernous room with only a piano and one or two judges, who are sometimes hidden behind a screen. A disembodied voice tells the contestant to "Begin" the two or three pieces she has worked on for months of solitary practice. The final notes bring a brusque, "Thank you," followed by hours of waiting to see if her name is on the winners' list.

Competitions such as these cause a zero-sum outcome. Even if a student wins, success seems related only to the whim of two sets of ears on any given day, and he doesn't even get to see those ears or the judges who own them!

As a teenager, the musical experience that spurred my best playing happened at music camp. For hours and hours I practiced Ravel's Concerto in G Major, continually striving for a higher and higher performance level because I heard my younger camp mate, Andrew Rangell, playing it with more mastery in the practice room next door. Rangell did indeed go on to earn a doctorate at Juilliard, received an Avery Fisher Career Grant, and became a Boston-based concert pianist.

Andy and I developed a friendly rivalry that included an exchange of technical and musical ideas about the piece. For a lark we staged a simultaneous performance of the piece surrounded by a group of our cheering fellow musicians. We didn't need criticism or praise, nor did one of us need to win. Our teacher, live performances, and recordings of the concerto had guided our ears and fingers toward a high-standard performance of the piece. The sound of the music itself, not outside praise or criticism, let us know how close we were to creating an optimal performance.

It helps to keep both praise and criticism to a minimum. If we provide a model for how a piece is supposed to sound, give technical and musical guidance, and sit with children as they learn to work and experience appropriate struggle, we will find ways to spark the engine of their own desire to master every piece they encounter. Students will learn to monitor their own progress. They will internally know whether both their effort and its result deserve A's or not.

Leaving both criticism and praise at the door, we can indulge in a different type of exclamation: "What beautiful music you are making!"

STICKERS, SKITTLES, AND M&M'S

One of my friends shared a story about her grandson's recent violin recital. Seven-year-old Peter's performance had gone well. Afterward, he ran to his father for a hug, but stopped short when he noticed another student and his family standing nearby. That boy's father was reaching into his wallet for a $20 bill, which he handed to his six-year old son. The boy's mother said, "Here is the reward we promised you for practicing. Now aren't you glad you did?" My friend's grandson tugged at his father's coat. "Hey, Dad, what do I get for playing in the recital?" "You get the pleasure of making beautiful music for all of us to enjoy," his father replied. Wise dad.

Over forty-six years of teaching, I have given out my fair share of stickers, stars, Skittles and M&M'S. I have made umpteen practice charts and have even let children choose a present for completing their AIM theory and performance exams. Did these extrinsic rewards work? Yes, but only in the short run. More often than not, the student spent more time choosing a sticker than playing a piece. I knew I had hit a dead end the year I challenged my students to practice an hour a day for a hundred consecutive days. Several of my students were so stunned by the magnitude of this assignment that they thought it deserved a huge reward. My student Patrick said it best. "Wow! That sounds hard! What will you give us for doing that—a computer?"

Author Jessica Lahey writes, "The use of rewards and incentives prioritizes scores and grades over exploration and experimentation, which undermines a teacher's ability to foster self-directed and intrinsically motivated learning."[1] My students who worked for an outside reward tended to choose shorter, easier pieces and were reluctant to move to higher AIM levels for fear they wouldn't get their prize. One summer I taught composition to middle-school music campers. During the first week of camp I promised several prizes for the completion of an assigned group composition project only to hear the lead student instruct the others: "Just copy down that I-V7-I progression in C major four times and write in some notes from the C major five-finger pattern for a melody. That way we will finish first and get the best choice for our prize."

Lahey points out: "Rewards don't work, because humans perceive them as attempts to control behavior, which undermines intrinsic motivation. Human beings are more likely to stick with tasks that arise out of their own free will and personal choice."[2] The second week of camp I offered no prizes, just a performance opportunity for the group that the class felt had worked the hardest and had created the most complex, inspiring piece. In addition, I gave them a choice of three sets of parameters for the proposed composition. The same group of children turned in a thirty-two-measure piece in ABA form that included a modulation from G major to D major as well as intricate rhythms that propelled some delightful twists and turns of melody.

Of course, there are exceptions. Trophies or diplomas offered as rites of passage fall into a different category. The Stanley Cup, Olympic medals, college diplomas, and similar prizes mark the end of long periods of work. They act as celebration for inner-directed work rather than minute-to-minute outside motivation to do a task someone else thinks they should do.

Children understand the folly of using stars and stickers better than we do. My colleague Phillip Keveren once told me this story about his then-four-year-old son, Sean. Phillip traveled a great deal, playing concerts and giving presentations. His son missed him so much that he carried around a puzzle piece from his United States map, whichever one represented the current state where his father was performing. Phillip and his wife, conscientious parents, had the proverbial list of daily tasks and chores posted on their kitchen wall. Sean and his sister pasted a star beside every completed activity, such as "brushing your teeth" or "feeding the dog." One morning Phillip's son came to him with a star chart he had made for his father. He announced that his father could now earn stars, too. Phillip expressed his admiration for the chart and asked, "What do I have to do to get a star?" His son looked him straight in the eye and said, "Be home when I wake up in the morning."

"I THOUGHT IT SOUNDED GREAT!"

Even if we soft-pedal both praise and criticism, how we appraise a child's work matters. As the renowned pedagogue Frances Clark used to say, "Be careful that your studio doesn't become a house of correction." We are partners in the child's learning and our reactions do matter—a lot.

Guiding a child toward an accurate view of her efforts begins with the first lesson. We immediately let children know we have knowledge and expertise to share when we show them how to sit at the piano and how to place their fingers on the keyboard. We also let them know that we trust their ability to monitor themselves if we turn the tables and pretend we are the student. Children love to tell you whether you are sitting up straight or playing with a proper hand position. "We know something only when we can teach it ourselves" has become a well-known adage for a reason.

The year I taught first graders in Apple Creek, Ohio, I invented the character Crazy Gertie. While that might not be a politically correct name in today's culture, the children loved her. (Her likeness, Mr. Noodle on *Sesame Street*, had not yet come on the air in 1968.) I told the students that if they completed their work with some speed, we would have time for her visit. At the appointed time, I "disappeared" into the hall and Crazy Gertie returned, complete with clodhopper shoes, a shawl, and a bandana.

Crazy Gertie couldn't get anything right. Her math equations didn't add up; she misspelled words; she sang out of tune. As long as they stayed in their seats, I allowed the children to call out her errors and to suggest corrections, which they did with much energy. Crazy Gertie often chose the child who was having the most trouble with the day's assignment to come to the front of the room and teach her "the right way." I was continually amazed at how expert the formerly confused child became.

For many years I began to comment the second a child stopped playing his assigned piece. Now I step back and ask the student to evaluate herself. "What went well that time?" Students find this an extremely difficult question to answer. They always begin to tell me what didn't go well. When I stop them and repeat my question, they often begin to fidget. I let silence fill the room. Eventually, they speak up in a shy voice and tell me what they liked about their performance.

As much as we praise children in an attempt to raise their self-esteem, they still feel it is something akin to bad manners to speak well of themselves. Yet I insist they do. I tell them, "Yes, yes. There were problems. We will get to those, but first let's celebrate what you did master."

I have another reason for asking this question. With some exceptions, children know exactly how well they did. This lets me know they have internalized what I have been teaching and that we can move on. When I talk less, they work more.

Once you coax students into telling you what went well, you can work together to discover why those portions of the piece were successful. This information will help them as they shift to the parts of the music that still need work. Again, they will sometimes do your teaching for you if you step back and listen. Students often not only know what went wrong, but also know how to answer my next question, "Do you have any ideas for ways to fix the problem?" Lots of times they do! I think, "Hooray, they did hear me!" Only when they look at me in genuine confusion or directly ask for help do I step in.

Students sometimes come up with unique solutions of their own. Meredith, an intelligent, hardworking nine-year-old, struggled with reading notes. No matter how I presented them, she labored from one note to the next. Once she had read a piece a few times, she played with physical ease and musicality. She didn't play by ear, which sometimes makes note-reading difficult; she simply couldn't grasp the location, direction, and distance of the notes.

One day Meredith stopped in the middle of her piece and said, "I have an idea. I have this same trouble with reading words and sentences at school. It helps if I write out every word. Why don't I write the name under every note?"

Because Meredith was playing at a late-elementary level, this sounded like a tedious process. In addition, I feared this overemphasis on note names would prevent her from reading well by intervals, motifs, and phrases. No one wants to grow up and have to write down every note name in a Beethoven sonata! I knew Meredith to be a wise child, though, so I agreed to let her try her idea.

Over the next several weeks, Meredith wrote in every note name in every one of her pieces. She had the additional idea of using a different color for each note—red for C's, for example. Her idea worked! Meredith's brain needed this physical step of writing down the information. She eventually stopped naming each note and wrote in each interval. In time she let go of both these aids and began reading with ease.

Sometimes it is best to teach by asking questions and sometimes it is best to impart knowledge by instructing. A wise teacher knows at what point in the lesson each is optimal. The late pedagogue

Lynn Olson used to teach using a primarily child-centered, Socratic method. By his own admission, he occasionally went too far in this direction. One day a young boy confirmed this by saying, "Mr. Olson, do we have to do whatever we want again today?" There are certain times when it is all right to use a method closer to "See that key? Just put your finger on it and play it!" Of course, a balance between the two is best.

Some students are too hard on themselves; nothing sounds good enough. Others look at you with a cheery smile and say, "I thought that sounded great," when it didn't. These children need extra guidance toward the reality of their performances. Most children, though, have an accurate idea of their progress and performance.

One afternoon, my nine-year-old student Sam had barely played the last note of his piece before his supportive mother said, "Oh, Sam, that was fantastic." In reality the music had been far less than perfect. Sam looked at his mother, then looked at me, and said, "Oh no! Should we tell her?"

PLATEAUS AND FALLOW PERIODS

Fallow periods. Farmers know every field needs them. The earth cannot sustain continuous growth. Why then do we humans think we can?

Unflagging effort creates steady progress, or so the story goes. Yet who among us is capable of unceasing work and ever-expanding growth? In addition, the instant communication of this twenty-first-century world heightens our expectations of continual creativity and connection. Political speeches, disasters, cute dog tricks—all loop endlessly on television and YouTube. *The New Yorker* once ran a cartoon that featured a world-weary couple sitting in front of their television. The husband says, "What shall we do tonight?" to which the wife answers, "Let's turn on CNN and see if there are any disasters."

The students currently studying in our studios were born sometime between 1993 and 2011. They never knew a time when cell phones and the Internet did not exist. I recently told Joey, one of my tech-addicted teenage students, about the time my former father-in-law accidentally cut the telephone line to Calvin Coolidge's summer home. Yes, the one telephone line.

During the summer of 1927, one specially dedicated phone line snaked its way through my father-in law's western Nebraska farm on its way to Rapid City, South Dakota, where Calvin and Grace

Coolidge were enjoying a three-month—yes, a three-month—fallow period in the Black Hills. All of the folks living along this wired connection between Coolidge and rest of the world knew which cable belonged to the president. One afternoon, while harvesting his wheat field, my father-in-law drove the top of his combine through the presidential wire. To his horror, he looked back to see the two broken ends of the wire hanging limply from their poles.

After running the entire two miles to his house, he confessed his error to his father, a man who had helped wire all of Fremont, Nebraska, for electricity. Together they raced back to the field, shinnied up the poles, reconnected the wire ends, and restored telephone service to the president. Over an hour had passed, and no one had noticed the interruption in service.

Joey's response: "You're kidding, right? You mean your father-in-law had to run all the way home? I can't imagine not having a cell phone with me!" He didn't even mention the unthinkable circumstance of a president having only one, unguarded telephone connection to the world.

I was telling fourteen-year-old Joey this story because he was experiencing a musical fallow period. He had practiced well and made reasonably steady progress for four years. Now, for whatever reason, he seemed unable to move to a new level. His technical facility had stalled out at an early-advanced level and his formerly musical way of playing had started to sound wooden. He was musician enough to know he was stuck, and he felt miserable. Music no longer sustained him; it felt like a burden.

My response to Joey: "Good. Let's enjoy this plateau. At least you know where you are. Let's honor this hiatus. Let's cut all connections and go underground to rest." We canceled his upcoming MTNA theory and performance exams; jettisoned all the pieces he was currently working on; and cleared his assignment book. He even decided not to take the job of choral accompanist at his high school, because he didn't enjoy the music they were singing. We started over—together.

I asked Joey to bring MP3s of three of his favorite pieces to his next lesson. Together we listened to Ivo Pogorelich's performance of *Für Elise*, John Mayer's "Waiting on the World to Change," and selections from Ramsey Lewis's *Songs from the Heart* album. I marveled at Joey's eclectic and excellent musical taste. For three more weeks we continued this approach, enjoying long talks about different composers, performers, and the music itself.

By the fourth week of our fallow period, Joey was itching to play the piano again. He had been picking out the John Mayer tune by ear, and had started adding an accompaniment. He asked for some help. Using the recorded performance as a guide, we drew on all of Joey's theoretical knowledge of chords, scales, and accompaniment styles as he began fashioning his own arrangement. Using the music's chords in the rhythm of the music's drum beat, he created a sophisticated accompaniment.

The next week Joey surprised me by singing along to the Mayer song as he played his now polished arrangement. Joey's mellow voice soared over the sound of the piano. Emotion filled every phrase. I asked him to sing it several more times to our shared enjoyment.

Joey tackled *Für Elise* next. He met me at the door for this lesson, eager to show me how he had used a YouTube tutorial to learn the A section of the piece. While his fingering, phrasing, and dynamics needed some correction, Joey had accurately taught himself the notes. We fixed these problems with ease. He then showed me a slightly jazzy interlude he had added to the Mayer song. Joey had always enjoyed improvising, but our careful listening to the song, including attempts to duplicate the drum rhythm and replicate the other instruments' lines, had inspired him. His interlude included melodic twists and a new harmonic refinement that signaled a blossoming originality.

The musical view from Joey's weeks in the fallow underground inspired both of us. He not only reconnected to the music he loved, he also taught both of us where his budding adult self wanted to go with his music. He returned to his piano study with new energy.

Students often need time to incorporate what they have learned. Concepts, technique, and musical maturity need to knit, to catch up with each other. As some of the only teachers who have students for a long period of time, we have the luxury of being able to sit with them while they absorb the music with all of their senses. Joey and I cut the wire that buzzed with the expectations of the outside world. Well over an hour passed and no one noticed.

TEACHING SIDEWAYS

In addition to fallow periods, when no progress seems to be happening, students sometimes need to stay at one level for what can seem like a long time. Their interest and practice time remain high, but they still find the newest concepts and techniques cumbersome. They need us to "teach sideways."

We teachers often get hung up on progress. We have made a lesson plan for the year and by gum we are going to stick to it! This child will be to Level III by May! We forget that learning happens in a spiral and not in a straight line. Some concepts and techniques come easily to a child. They can move to the next unit or piece with ease. Others trip them up. These periods call for additional repertoire at the same level. Easy-sounds-hard pieces for example, allow students to combine all they have learned before adding new information.

Also, children who enter a period where they want to play only one style of music, will eventually move on. Trust the music. Middle-school students often make what seems like a prolonged attachment to a specific musical style. It is important to step back and allow this to happen. My student Tommy spent his sixth-grade year playing seven theme songs from James Bond movies (thank goodness for Dan Coate's technically demanding and authentic arrangements of this music). We made recordings of Tommy's performances for his grandfather, who loved the Bond movies. He would pop Tommy's recordings into his car tape deck and enjoy them as he drove around the city. The music provided a close connection between the two at an important time in Tommy's life. By the beginning of seventh grade, Tommy was ready via Scott Joplin to add Mozart and Grieg to his popular music repertoire.

When mothers of two-year-olds worry about the progress of their toddler's potty training, I remember a wise friend of mine who used to say, "Get a grip. Every child is potty trained by the time they go to college." In other words, take the long view.

How can we tell when a student has finished a piece? Maybe the answer is: "Never." How many of us played Beethoven's "Waldstein" Sonata up to a certain level, put a sticker on it, and then moved on? We didn't. Instead we play this piece and others like it throughout our lives, returning to them over and over as our technique and maturity grow and as our emotional understanding changes.

The same is true for children's music. From the third lesson on I assign "Mystery Tunes." Part of the child's assignment is to choose two or three already-learned pieces and to play them for me at the next lesson. Due to time constraints, older students choose only one piece or one movement of a work. Yes, *they* choose the music! I leave blank spaces in their assignment books and ask them to write in the name of each selection.

At the end of the lesson the child plays these pieces for me. The little ones make me guess the names of each one. Most of the time I can! I do not comment on their performances. I simply listen to and enjoy them. If they need guidance or if something in the music needs correction, we return to the piece at the beginning of the next lesson.

Why do I do this? First of all, I want my students to leave the lesson remembering that they can play something well. After the struggle of teaching a new concept, it helps me remember, too. One of my students even remarked, "I remember when I had a lot of trouble learning this old piece, but I have it now." This encouraged both of us, who had spent the last fifteen minutes grappling with a new technical difficulty.

Secondly, it gives children a chance to keep polishing already-learned repertoire. Rather than staying with one piece until it is perfect (which might take several months), we can move on when the piece sounds "good enough," knowing we will return to it again and again as their increasing expertise makes it easier and easier to play.

Of course, students don't return to every piece. This is the third reason I assign Mystery Tunes: students' favorite-piece choices teach me what music most appeals to them. My students often surprise me. Eleven-year-old Lesley was working on her first Mozart sonata. When it came time for her to play her Mystery Tune, she pulled out an old gem: Edna Mae Burnam's *Dozen a Day, Book 2*, a volume she had completed in her second year of study. "I am going to play all of these exercises in 12 keys," she announced. I glanced at my watch. "Well, not all of them, of course, but I finally get this transposition stuff!" She did, too. Over the next three lessons, she did indeed transpose the entire book.

My eight-year-old student Allie was studying pieces from Bartok's *Mikrokosmos, Book Two*. One afternoon she surprised her mother and me by playing Phillip Keveren's hauntingly beautiful, slow arrangement of "Twinkle, Twinkle Little Star," a piece from her first year of study. Allie's heartfelt performance brought us to tears. We sat in silence for a while before Allie said, "You know why I played that piece today, don't you?" We said, "No." She answered, "It's the tenth anniversary of the *Challenger* explosion."

Then there was Lily. Lily studied piano for five years. Before every lesson and at every recital she included a performance of Phillip Keveren's "Water Lily," an off-staff piece from her first method book. "It's my signature tune," she would explain.

PERFECTLY MANAGING IMPERFECTION

Here's a slight twist on Dr. Thomas Harris's 1976 self-help book, *I'm OK. You're OK*— I'm Not OK. You're Not OK. And That's OK. Another way to say it: Life is perfect because it is perfectly what it is.

Today's flawless recordings create unrealistic expectations. We now assume we will hear and create perfect live performances. We fail to remember that, in the recording studio, every note and dynamic shading is fine-tuned. Mistakes are edited out without leaving a trace. YouTube allows us listen to old recordings of iconic pianists with the wave of a finger. Schnabel, Rubinstein, Neuhaus—the list goes on. My students are amazed when they hear these artists play a smudged note or a blurred run. They also admit that the performances, imperfect as they sometimes are, astound and engage them.

I once played the Mozart Trio in Eb, K. 498 at a Ravinia master class taught by Janos Starker and Rudolf Büchbinder. Büchbinder served as my page turner, hovering over me as I played and dropping ash from his lit cigarette onto the bass keys. Starker, the lead teacher, spent nearly half an hour on ways to unify the turn in the opening phrase of the first movement. His intense—I think they were green—eyes terrified me.

As I walked away from the stage, an older man came up to

me and said, "For my money, the Mozart was the most beautiful performance today." Being a young graduate student, I began to list my "mistakes." I guess I wanted him to know I was aware the performance was imperfect, that my standards were higher. The man stopped me mid-sentence, touched my arm, and said, "Ah, but nothing perfect has ever moved me." He turned and walked away. I later learned the man was Starker's father.

Mistakes in performance are unfortunate but human. Mistakes in practice are necessary! In his book *The Perfect Wrong Note*, William Westney says, "The golden pathway to learning, not just in music but in anything in life, is through one's own, individual mistakes."[1] And remember, Coyle's research: "In order to get your skill circuit to fire optimally, you must by definition fire the circuit sub-optimally; you must make mistakes and pay attention to those mistakes; you must slow teach your circuit."[2]

Westney distinguishes between honest and careless mistakes. "How can you tell? If you weren't paying attention at the time and you didn't take the mistake seriously and deal with it immediately—telling yourself—'This never happened before; I just wasn't concentrating; well, nobody's perfect; even Babe Ruth struck out a lot; sounds pretty good on the whole; I know this perfectly well—I don't know why I got so nervous!'—then it is a careless mistake, a mistake that will cause you trouble later on, just as we've always been told. But if you *were* paying attention and the mistake happened anyway, it's probably honest. Honest mistakes aren't caused by inattention; they're simply what happens when the body is allowed to express itself without restriction. If you take time immediately to process that mistake, your learning will be pure and lasting."[3]

When I was the camp practice partner, I often saw the markings teachers made in their student's music. Chronic mistakes earned check marks, hastily scrawled stars, arrows, and the ubiquitous circles, often in red ink. One teacher circled the cadence in a Bach invention so often that she tore right through the music. I have made all of these worthless marks in my day.

Because I practiced with children every day, I watched them wrestle with inaccuracies. Some were ingrained and regularly occurred at the places marked; others showed up willy-nilly, like a thunderstorm on a cloudless day.

When I heard a mistake, I often stopped the student and said, "Don't look at the music. Tell me what note you are supposed to be playing there." Nearly every time the student answered by naming the wrong note she had just played! "So you didn't play a mistake," I would say. "You played exactly what you thought the music indicated." They always looked surprised.

"Look again," I would say. "What note do you see?" "Oh, it's a different note," they would exclaim. Immediately, the mistake disappeared. Practice sessions became ones of curiosity, not frustration.

A similar result happened when students encountered a technical difficulty they could not master. Rather than running over the passage again and again, hoping it would work this time, we would stop. I would ask, "How does your body look when it is playing that passage? (Now I use my iPad to video them.) Sometimes they realized they were sitting too close to the keyboard or their shoulders were hunched, or their arm needed to follow their fingers more closely. Whatever the solution, it became one of experiment rather than mindless repetition. Repetition is important, but is valuable only after the notes and rhythms are accurate and the body is moving comfortably!

My student Sarah taught me that some mistakes exist because students like them. Sarah loved the composer Bob Vandall's Prelude No. 4. Yet the middle section, particularly the cadence, bedeviled her. Week after week, no matter how often we examined the music and her technical approach to it, she played wrong notes and rhythms.

One day Sarah stopped and said, "I just don't like the way that passage sounds!" I realized she wasn't commenting on her errors. She actually didn't like the way the music was written. "How would you compose that section if it were your prelude?" I asked. Sarah, an ardent composer and improviser, brightened, "I think it would sound more beautiful this way!" She demonstrated. Indeed, the "wrong" notes sounded beautiful in their own right. I acknowledged this.

"Let's call Mr. Vandall," I said. Sarah played her version of the much-maligned passage over the telephone. (This was in the old days.) Bob liked the sound of her "improvisation" and complimented Sarah on her musical taste. He then said, "Now play it my way!" Sarah laughed. As a composer she understood that no one likes to have his music changed. What surprised all of us? Sarah then played the original version perfectly!

Of course, performance brings its own challenges. I tell my students, "The only mistake you can make in a performance is to stop. Play something. Play anything, but don't stop!" Of course, it is best if the performer can play notes that sound like they belong in the piece, but something is better than nothing. When students are preparing for a recital, we play a game. They begin their piece. At some point I interrupt and say, "Improvise!" The student shifts to her own ideas, making them as stylistically close to the original music as possible. After a few measures, I say, "Resume!" and they return to the original notes. No matter how carefully we prepare a piece, nerves can cause us to wander from the score. It helps to know that we can improvise our way out of these moments and leave the stage with our head held high.

FAILURE: IT'S A STRENGTH

My childhood teacher entered her students, including me, in many contests. When I was fifteen, I performed in the Nebraska Music Teachers' Association state competition: the Prelude from Bach's English Suite No. 2 in A Minor and the first movement of Beethoven's Sonata Op. 2 No. 3. The Bach went well enough, but while playing the Beethoven, I blanked out during several measures of the recapitulation, playing some stray-sounding notes and then rushing through the coda, eager to get offstage.

As we waited for the results, my father sat silently beside me. Surprisingly, the judges asked two of us to return to the stage: a young man playing a Chopin nocturne and myself. They wanted to hear the Beethoven again. I proceeded to play it well until the same pesky measures, where I again wandered into unknown territory. The other contestant played better than he had the first time and won the competition.

While I wasn't devastated, I was disappointed. It would almost have been better if I had not come so close. On the two-hour drive home, my father still said nothing until we neared our house. He then sighed and said, "They always choose the boy. The boy always wins." While I suppose he said this to lessen my dejection or to lighten any blame I might put on myself, it had the opposite effect. I could secure my performances by practicing harder and studying my music more closely. I couldn't, however, become a boy.

The following year I won first place in the same state competition. While my father was happy, my teacher was not. "I had hoped Elsa would win," she said. She is more prepared for the divisional and national rounds. While this was true, this comment didn't exactly shore up my confidence. In addition, my mother did not want me to go onto the next rounds of the competition, because I would have to practice too much. She thought this would wear me out. She was also about to give birth to my sister, and she didn't want my practice to disturb her or the baby. In the divisional competition, held in Chicago that year, I didn't even place.

Obviously, I wasn't entering these competitions because of my own motivation. If I had, others' comments and needs wouldn't have sent me off track so easily. I would have stuck to my guns. Unfortunately, these less-than-positive experiences influenced my own teaching and parenting in the early years. I was determined not to let any of my students or my own children fail.

This is neither a reasonable nor a laudable goal. Angela Duckworth, a McArthur fellow, says, "Failure strengthens grit like no other factor,"[1] and it is a person's grit that determines her ability to succeed. When Thomas Edison failed over and over again to bring the lightbulb into existence, he said, "I have not failed. I've just found 10,000 ways that won't work."

In her book *The Gift of Failure*, Jessica Lahey writes, "History is filled with stories of extraordinary people, inventors and innovators, who learned how to appropriate the gifts of failure to their own advantage, who did not run from it, but stayed in its company long enough to become comfortable among the jumbled wreckage of their dashed hopes and failed plans."[2]

When my eleven-year-old son failed by one point the placement exam that would allow him to begin taking high-school math courses in sixth grade, I was upset. My son sat me down for a talk.

"When I am 35, it won't matter whether I failed this test or not. Besides, I did fairly well on it. You only want me to go to the high school early so you can say you have a smart son."

Ouch.

Over the years Ben taught me that I do have a smart son indeed, in all the ways that matter. He was right. He now works as vice president of information technology, a highly mathematical job, for a major movie and television studio.

Lahey says, "Parents, after all, are judged by their children's accomplishments rather than their happiness, so when our children fail, we appropriate those failures as our own."[3]

It is unwise, and, yes, damaging to look to our children and students to make us look good as parents and teachers. Michael Thompson says, "We all want to feel competent as parents and that means when things aren't going right, our impulse is to jump in and fix them. . . . American parents, in particular, do not trust development. They want to make it happen; they want to push it or feel they are controlling it. . . . There is a useful distinction . . . between being impatient with development and believing that it is something you can engineer like a hybrid soybean. You can create a good growing space for a child . . . but you can't make development happen."[4]

My desire to protect my son from failure had been around long before he was eleven. Yes, I wanted to say I had a smart son so I would look good as a parent, but remembering my own unresolved failures, I also wanted to protect both of my children from all disappointment and hurt. Fortunately, Ben had a wise first-grade teacher in Mary Hunter. At our first parent-teacher conference, she listened quietly as I worried out loud about my son's reading level, his math skills, his social interactions. When I finally stopped talking, she took my hand in hers and said, "Now you leave that boy alone. He is just fine, just fine the way he is." Obviously, I didn't learn the lesson then, but I think it was her unconditional regard for my son that gave him the strength to confront me quietly five years later and for me to hear him.

Lahey again: "Failure—from small mistakes to huge miscalculations—is a necessary and critical part of our children's development. Failure is too often characterized as a negative: an F in math or a suspension from school. However, all sorts of disappointments, rejections, corrections, and criticism are small failures, all opportunities in disguise, valuable gifts misidentified as tragedy."[5]

Of course, we do not want to set children up for unnecessary failure. It is up to us as teachers to prepare our students adequately for upcoming performances and to help them determine whether they are ready or not to perform a given piece. When ten-year-old Rosie decided she wanted to play an arrangement of "The Trepak Dance," which was one level above her current skill, I decided to let her do it. Rosie is a serious skater, who hopes one day to skate the role of Clara in our community's annual Christmas ice show. Remember that desire equals success.

Two red flags presented themselves, though. First, the January recital was only two months away and Rosie would be busy skating a duet in the ice show and then going on a two-week skiing trip over the holidays. Secondly, Rosie usually played two pieces in the recital and her mother was determined that she should do that again this year.

Rosie and I discussed these obstacles. After some reflection, she still wanted to play the piece. I also sat down with Rosie's mother and showed her how much more difficult the piece was than Rosie's current music, and told her I celebrated Rosie's desire to take on the music's difficulty. I informed her that, because of the piece's complexity and length, Rosie and I had agreed that she would be playing only one piece on the recital. While not happy with this decision, the mother stood aside.

Rosie worked hard and with determination. As the recital approached, however, two phrases of the piece still eluded her. A week before the performance, with Rosie's help, I slightly simplified the arrangement, sacrificing nothing in sound, but making the piece more playable in a week's time. I told Rosie she would still need to work hard, but I believed she could master the music. She did it! Unfortunately, in the end her mother failed to see that she had accomplished a big leap in her learning and preparation. She thought Rosie wasn't progressing quickly enough and should quit lessons because she had played only one work and not two like her friends had done.

Was this success or failure? Did I make the right decision? I think I did, despite the fact that the mother ended Rosie's lessons and signed her up for more ice-skating time. Rosie chose her own goal and reached it through hard work. I believe she ignited her own desire to work and to succeed. She played well. She wanted to continue her study. I still teach other children in the family and my hope is that Rosie will someday return to lessons.

At the same recital, my outstanding student Corey ran off the rails during Chopin's "Minute Waltz." A busy young man of thirteen, Corey had prepared well, but had simply run out of time. With two more weeks of practice, Corey would have been more securely prepared. We sat down and discussed his readiness for performance. At that point the piece often went extremely well, but at other times, because it was not completely cured, Corey had difficulty. I asked him if he would like save the Waltz for a later recital and substitute a jazz piece with improvisation, one he had studied earlier in the semester and knew well. He wanted to play the Chopin. At the recital, Corey did have some difficulty, but he still played the piece with flair and beauty. A good improviser, he simply made up some notes and went on during the rocky section.

While the audience and his family were a little surprised, because Corey almost always plays without incident, everyone complimented his efforts and risk-taking and Corey said, "I am going to go home and work on that section over and over until I can depend on it. Can I play it again in the next recital?" I assured him that we would love to hear it again. In this case, I think Corey would have felt like he had failed if he had chosen the safer jazz piece and played it perfectly.

Lahey says, "Self-imposed goals are the safest place for a child to fail"[6] Also, "Lots of kids can ace a test using plan A, but it's going to be the kid who has tried and failed and regrouped . . . to try again with twenty-five other plans who will create true innovation and change in our world."[7]

When children's best efforts sometimes fail, it is wise simply to sit with them. Just quietly listening to a child can be healing. It is best not to gloss over the failure or to blame someone or something else for it. Let them own it. Let them know you, too, have failed at times in your life and that you grew stronger from the experience.

When a child wants to take on a seemingly risky task, point out reality, then sit back and let them take the leap. If they succeed, we are there to celebrate with them. If they fail, we are there to commend their effort and resilience and to cheer them on as they try again.

ANOTHER LOOK AT SUCCESS

Everyone understands the success of winning a competition or performing well. The student and teacher pose for photos. Parents stand beaming nearby. I always enjoy that experience. What aren't obvious are the successful day-to-day achievements our less-visible students make.

Mallory studied with me for four years. Over ten years I taught all four children in her fine, supportive family. Mallory, the youngest, found it difficult to read music. Although she was a good athlete, her fingers moved hesitantly over the keyboard. Rhythmic concepts came slowly. During the first year I thought I was going to lose her.

Yet I had noticed two things about Mallory: she told me about her day with colorful descriptions and lots of humor, and she and the family Labrador, Moses, had a close relationship. One afternoon I put the method book away and asked her if she would like to make up a song about Moses. She actually jumped off the bench in excitement. "How will I do that?"

Fortunately, Mallory was studying a first-level piece that was an actual song with words. It had four phrases. Using the words as a template, I asked Mallory to substitute new ones about Moses. She did this with breathtaking ease! In fact, she had so much to say that she created four verses. Because the words were coming so quickly, I wrote them down for her. I then assigned her the task of copying and editing them to her final liking.

The following week, I guided Mallory as she used the five-finger pattern of the original song to make a melody to fit the song's words. She was so involved in this activity that she was sorry to see the lesson come to an end. By the third week, Mallory had created a song that was rhythmically and melodically more complex than the original method-book piece. The words were also much funnier. Best of all, she played her own piece beautifully.

When we returned to the original song, Mallory played it easily, although she now dismissed it as "boring." She liked her own piece better. Her reading still felt difficult on first try, and she was sometimes as frustrated as before, but she now had a way into the music that worked for her.

Mallory began composing B sections for some of her assigned pieces. None was more successful than one she created for Phillip Keveren's languid piece "Water Colors." At the spring recital Mallory played her "Moses" piece along with "Water Colors." Other students her age had progressed far faster and played more difficult repertoire, but Mallory had the audience in her pocket. She asked me to print the words to "Moses" on the recital program. Everyone laughed as she sang and played, and she brought tears to everyone's eyes with "Water Colors." I doubt anyone would have guessed what a success Mallory had created for herself, but I knew.

Mallory's progress continued to be slow, but she and Moses always greeted me at the door, Mallory with a smile and Moses with a lick. We both celebrated the creativity and insight Mallory brought to her music no matter how long it took her to learn each song. Once Mallory reached junior high, it was clear that playing the piano was not her best talent. Volleyball won out. Yet music had allowed Mallory a way for her to express her unique humor and insight and to develop the confidence to share herself with an audience. How lucky I was to join her in it.

As a six-year-old, Zoe always came to her lessons dressed in striking garb of her own choice. One of her favorite combinations included socks of two different patterns. Long, colorful scarves tied in contorted ways were another fashion statement. In fact, Zoe loved scarves so much that she kept one in my piano bench. At every lesson she swirled it around in a dance as I played her currently assigned piece. Zoe's creativity spilled out of her so fast, both verbally and physically, that it was a challenge to keep her focused on actually playing the piano.

Over time Zoe did well enough, but she had a hyper-extension of all of her muscles, fingers included. This made for slow-going technically. I fully expected her to stop lessons. I am certain many folks remembered what Zoe wore to the recitals, but I doubt they remember her performances well. Then Zoe hit junior high. Many students quit at this point, but Zoe caught fire. Many students resist studying for the AIM theory and performance exams. Zoe decided these were an exciting challenge.

For the next six years, Zoe studiously worked her way through level nine, playing increasingly technically difficult and intellectually challenging repertoire. Due to her hyper-elasticity we had to be careful as she mastered scales, arpeggios, and Hanon. One semester we had to stop lessons while she recovered from an injury she sustained while learning to type. She returned with eagerness, though, and amazed me at every turn with her accomplishments. She even chose to spend two summers at music camp.

No, Zoe was not destined to become a music major or a performer; she became a writer like her father. Yet the day her parents and I best celebrated her musical success was the day her mother came to me and said, "Zoe just interviewed at the college of her choice. Her first question was, 'Is there a piano in the dorm? I play every day and I absolutely have to have access to one.'"

Part Four

TEACHING
YOURSELF

BEING COMFORTABLE
IN YOUR TEACHER SKIN

We music teachers work at our profession despite society's opinion of us. Maggie Smith's portrayal of a piano teacher in the movie *A Private Function* is a less-than-positive one that matches many people's view. The movie takes place in rural England during the time of heavy World War II rationing. Smith, the socially ambitious wife of a local podiatrist, teaches piano at their modest home. Every teaching scene shows the same uninspired young girl poking at the piano keys and playing one excruciating mistake after the other at an agonizingly slow tempo. Smith simply wanders around the living room looking pained and making impatient and rude comments to the girl, who always packs up her music and runs out of the house at the first opportunity, only to return the following week sounding exactly the same.

This movie is only one example! The animated movie *Inside Out* features an eleven-year-old hockey player, who is moving with her family from Minneapolis to San Francisco. The child's emotional memory bank is depicted as a series of different-colored balls (blue for sad, for instance) stacked side-by-side in long, winding rows. One scene presents two janitorial types, who are cleaning out the young girl's fading, less-significant emotions to create more room for new ones. At one point we hear one of them say, "Seven years of piano lessons! Those can go. Keep 'Chopsticks' and 'Heart and Soul' and get rid of the rest!"

In addition, how many of us have answered the question, "What do you do?" only to have the questioner launch into either a harrowing description of his own tortured piano lessons or a sad revelation of her regret at having quit because she hated practicing.

Are we really this awful? Of course not. I do think, though, that as music teachers we bring some of this negative reaction on ourselves. For example, we continually answer the what-do-you-do question with the phrase, "I 'play' the piano." The word "play" suggests that to do so is an easy skill. We often say we "teach piano." This is actually an odd phrase if you think about it. In addition, we do not contradict people who say, "Oh, you have musical talent, I don't." This gives the mistaken idea that music flows out of us without effort, that we have been tapped by the music gods. We also think of ourselves as artists, who might somehow be corrupted by also being business persons. Worst of all, we apologize for what we charge and we don't charge enough! (This fact requires a separate chapter to follow.)

Long ago I switched to these answers: "I am a musician who teaches children and adults," and "I am a pianist." I also say, "I teach children and adults to become musicians who are pianists." Words matter and this slight shift of emphasis makes a difference in how people see us. I also point out that math requires special talent, too, but it is the hard work of learning both music and math that makes us successful.

Despite others' sometimes negative view of music teachers, those of us who are independent teachers have led a privileged life. Public school teachers, who are now criticized more than ever, have not been as lucky.

In her book *The Teacher Wars: A History of America's Most Embattled Profession*, Dana Goldstein writes:

Teachers have been embattled by politicians, philanthropists, intellectuals, business leaders, social scientists, activists on both the Right and Left, parents, and even one another. . . . Americans have debated who should teach public school; what should get taught; and how teachers should be educated, trained, hired, paid, evaluated, and fired. Though we've been arguing about these questions for two centuries, very little consensus has developed.[1]

I began my teaching career as a public-school teacher assigned to a troubled school on the West Side of Philadelphia, Pennsylvania, during the historic school year of 1967–'68. I taught third grade. That year both Martin Luther King and Bobby Kennedy were assassinated, and 164 civil disorders occurred in 128 American cities, including Detroit, Newark, and Philadelphia. I arrived in the City of Brotherly Love to find the neighborhood near Belmont School, my first teaching home, still smoldering from the summer's riots. During that year I met some outstanding, committed, and yes, heroic teachers. I also met some beautiful children who were already scarred, scared, and in need. I remember every one of them vividly.

Recently, I looked up the statistics for Belmont School. While the institution is now a charter school, the students are still underperforming. Great Schools, an independent, nonprofit organization and the leading national source of school information for families, rated Belmont Charter School as a two out of ten. Using the Pennsylvania System of State Assessments, in 2012, 46 percent of grade three students were performing at or above grade level and 40 percent were at or above grade level in reading. My heart hurt when I read this news.

Beginning in 1969, I elected out of the world of public-school teaching and began my career as an independent music teacher. My former husband's need to take an academic position at The College of Wooster in the bucolic Ohio countryside made my decision not to return to the embattled world of urban public education one over which I had no choice. Yet I still remember my guilt mixed with relief.

Goldstein says:

> *Many extraordinary men and women worked in public school classrooms and offered powerful, grass-roots ideas for how to improve American education. Henry David Thoreau, Susan B. Anthony, W.E.B. DuBois, and Lyndon B. Johnson are just a few of the famous Americans who taught. They resisted the fantasy of educators as saints or saviors, and understood teaching as a job in which the potential for children's intellectual transcendence and social mobility, though always present, is limited by real-world concerns such as poor training, low pay, inadequate supplies, inept administration, and impoverished students and families.[2]*

As an independent teacher, I have enjoyed a career free from the outside constraints often imposed on public school educators. In addition, I am the CEO of my own business. We independent teachers benefit from the following advantages. We can:

- teach as many or as few students as we wish
- determine our own rate of pay
- set our own schedule
- design our own curriculum
- live where we want
- design our own teaching space
- combine teaching with other jobs, either music-related or not
- be flexible during economic downturns
- control our own retirement plans and investments
- adjust quickly to cultural, societal, and technological changes

- work for as many years as we want
- share our students' lives for many years

Over the course of my career I have expanded and contracted my studio according to my needs and those of my family. When my children were young, I taught in my home studio and at the preparatory department at Northwestern University. A babysitter took care of my son and daughter during my teaching hours, but I was nearby should they need me. Once they were in late middle school and early high school, I cut my number of students from forty-five to twenty and took an additional full-time job as the Editor of *Clavier* magazine. When my children were in college, I cut my student load to two and commuted to another city to work for Hal Leonard Corporation, a major music-publishing company. After ten years of a three-hour, round-trip commute and extensive travel to give workshops all over the United States, Canada, the United Kingdom, Asia, Australia, and New Zealand, I quit my full-time job at the publishing company. I worked for them part-time as a consultant and re-expanded my home studio to fifty students. I now teach fifteen students in their homes, give workshops, and do a lot of writing.

The teachers I encounter at my workshops have similar work histories. Some teach in schools during the day and in their studios in the evenings and on weekends. Many are church musicians. Others combine non-musical jobs with their teaching. Over the years I have encountered many real estate agents, physical therapists, and nurses. Less common, but still frequent occupations are those of flight attendant or business manager/bookkeeper for a family farm or business. In Australia I met a piano teacher who was also a dentist! Of course, many teachers gig as performers and accompanists.

As independent teachers, we can live wherever we want and design our studios to fit our own dreams. We can teach at a school, a music store, at home, or in a music school of our own. We can work alone or with others. The new generation of teachers has moved from thinking of themselves as members of a home-based cottage industry to being the owners of a music business. They are founding full-fledged music schools that teach not only piano but also other instruments and voice. They teach all ages and teach for longer hours. For example, preschool and recreational music-making programs for older adults allow them to expand their teaching schedules into the mornings, early afternoons, and evenings. They also offer online classes that expand the boundaries of their studios. These new entrepreneurs teach all styles of music and include many performance opportunities, not only as chamber musicians and choir members but also as rock and jazz artists in bands, theater performers, and singer-songwriters.

When cultural, societal, and technological changes occur, we independent teachers can adapt quickly. We don't need to wait for someone else to approve changes in our business model or to provide us with materials. While economic downturns do affect us, it is my experience that parents are more likely to value music for their children in times of stress. My adult population also swells during recessions.

Best of all, we have the luxury of working one-on-one with students for several years of their lives. While not every student stays from preschool to high school, many do. Even those who shift from piano lessons to other activities usually study for a minimum of three or four years. I am currently teaching two grand-students, children of students I taught in my first years of teaching.

Recently I found myself discussing my work with a stranger on a plane. "I love what I do," I said. "Really? Wow, that's a rare thing to hear. I can't say that about my work. What do you do?" When I told him, he said, "But you can't make a good living at that, can you?" "Well," I replied, "I have more than managed to do so. I can't tell you I have made a wealthy living, but I have been living a wealthy life."

PAY YOURSELF A LIVING WAGE

Kristin Yost's book, *How I Made $100,000 My First Year as Piano Teacher*, made a well-deserved splash in 2011. After receiving her master's degree in piano performance and pedagogy from Southern Methodist University, Yost set up a studio in an affluent Dallas suburb. She convinced her parents to help her purchase a house, bought a first-class grand piano, and enrolled seventy students the first year!

Yost recruited this large number of students by thinking big and making a business plan right away. While not everyone may be able to buy a house, Yost makes the point that an apartment simply won't do. Shared musical walls make bad neighbors. If you can't buy, she suggests you rent. She also hired someone to make a splashy, interactive website, purchased high-quality business cards, and set a fee that would give her a living wage. To avail herself of more start-up cash, she took out a small-business loan.

Yost had also researched the neighborhood she chose for her studio. It included highly educated parents with high salaries who valued education and would value her philosophy of teaching. Yet even if teachers choose to live in a less-affluent area, they can do well if they first make a business plan and then stick to it. Their fee may be less than parents in an affluent area can pay, but their living expenses will be lower, too. In addition, I have met many teachers who live in underserved rural areas. Students drive many miles from surrounding towns, often filling these teachers' studios to the bursting point. I once met a New Zealand teacher who lived on a remote sheep farm. She taught eighty students!

Whether we have a home studio or a large music school, we piano teachers do not charge enough! Keep in mind that other after-school activities often charge hefty fees and have strict financial policies. In my community of Evanston, Illinois, it costs between $3,500 and $4,000 a year to play hockey (I am not including the cost of equipment); $1,400 a year to join the YMCA swim team; $900 a year for once-a-week dance lessons in a group of ten (the school suggests children take a minimum of two lessons a week); and $1,650 a year to study piano at a renowned music institute. Check out the cost of activities in your community and set your rate accordingly. I have.

These activities also include strict attendance policies. Hockey and swimming practices cannot be made up. Dance students may make up a missed lesson by joining another class, which may be at their level or lower. The music institute allows only one make-up lesson per semester and only in the event of illness or death in the family. No group lessons can be made up. I allow only two make-up lessons per year, which I give during the scheduled make-up week at the end of the school year.

Yost says, "As an entrepreneur, piano teachers have a marketing hat, a branding hat, an IT department hat, a customer service hat, an accounting hat and even a teacher hat! . . . As a teacher, you have so much knowledge, from pedagogical literature to philosophy, but you also need to have the knowledge about how to run a business, particularly a successful one."[1]

As someone who began teaching in the early '70s, I have seen the business of teaching change over time. In the early days of my studio, I did have the good sense to charge tuition by semester rather than a lesson-by-lesson fee, but I also taught at a school that failed to pay us until the parents paid. Sometimes I wouldn't get my first-semester check until late November! Even then, I received only the fees from the weeks I had already taught and not for the entire semester. The school portioned out the rest of the payment week by week. Also, I continually failed to solve the problem of reduced summer income. Despite sponsoring summer group lessons that included field trips to local concerts, I always felt like Mother Hubbard in August.

Yost has two hard and fast rules about tuition: "Clients pay by semester . . . and late payment (10 days) results in termination. Period. Not a late fee—termination."[2] I couldn't agree with her more. Yost also suggests hiring someone else to send out bills and collect tuition, even if it is a high-school student. Yost hired her sister, who lived 1,000 miles away. "She would correspond with people who were late in their tuition installments and she would implement fines. It is very difficult for the face of the teacher to be the face of the bill collector." That separation made Yost's life less stressful, "and parents were more respectful in the long run."[3]

Long ago I solved the problem of summer income in two ways. All students have to study for at least four weeks, although they may choose from many options, both private and group. I tack on this four-week charge to their spring tuition. Those who choose not to study at all (I have had this happen only once) know they must pay for the added four weeks to keep their place on my student roster. In August, I charge an enrollment fee for the following year. This fee includes payment for music, which I provide throughout the year, and for recitals, AIM exams, and any contests they might enter. August cupboard filled. Some smart teacher suggested this solution in an excellent *Keyboard Companion* article years ago. I wish I remembered her name!

Recently a student and her mother came to me for an interview.

In preparation for the visit, I had directed her to my website, which clearly states my tuition fee and all of my policies. As the interview came to its end, the mother said, "We would love to choose you as our teacher, but I am not used to paying this much money for piano lessons." Somewhat stunned, I said nothing. The mother filled the awkward silence with her request for a reduced fee. By that time I had found my voice, "I assume you read my qualifications. I charge a fee commensurate with my experience and with other teaching institutes in the area. I do not reduce my fee except in the case of teaching three or more children in one family." "Oh", she said, "I don't know what we can do." I knew this woman was a success-ful lawyer and that her daughter took ice-skating lessons and also played on a traveling hockey team. I said, "Well, I am sorry, too. I have so enjoyed meeting you and your daughter and hope you find her a teacher who is more affordable." They left.

Two days later the mother called me to schedule a lesson time for her daughter. She has been studying with me for three years.

PARENTS AS PARTNERS

In her book *The Gift of Failure*, Jessica Lahey writes, "Why do so many teachers cite the challenge of dealing with their students' parents as their main reason for abandoning the classroom?"[1] Throughout the public and private school systems, the relationship between parents and teachers has never ebbed lower. "Early in the evolution of our (American) educational system, open discussion between parents and teachers was the norm, and students graduated from one skill to the next rather than one grade to the next. However, as we moved to a standardized system of differentiation by age, and report cards replaced interpersonal communication, the divide between home and school widened."[2]

It is wise to see parents as partners, not problems. In the current public and private school atmosphere, this is a difficult view to maintain. As independent teachers, however, we have the luxury of sidestepping legislators, administrators, and lobbyists and can foster a relationship between teacher and parent more like the earlier version Lahey mentions. In some small way, our freedom from the pressures of mandated testing and curriculums may allow us to steer parents toward a more positive way of evaluating and supporting their children. Remember, my son's first-grade teacher did that for me!

Over the years, the vast majority of my parents has been not only respectful and supportive, but has also brought the joy of their friendship into my life. Yet different parents have different goals. It is important to identify these goals early on and to work as a team to fulfill not only the parents' expectations, but more importantly, those that fit the needs of the child. I have students who are serious classical musicians, singer-songwriters, jazz pianists, accompanists, and composers. A few have chosen music as a profession; all have chosen music as a lifetime passion. Most of my parents have been happy to support their children in these different musical vocations and avocations.

All parents want what they think is best for their child. All of them. Yet sometimes we don't agree on what that best looks like, and we teachers have to decide if and when to speak up.

I once received a call from an unusually realistic mother. She introduced herself and said, "Four of us want to learn how to play the piano. We are all beginners. I will probably start out and then get discouraged and quit. My oldest child, Judson, is a dancer. He is the most musical of us and will probably do fairly well and continue for a few years. Zach is slightly less interested, but will do okay. Lily, our youngest, is a first-class soccer player. She will enjoy lessons, do moderately well, and will quit when soccer begins to take more and more of her time."

Her scenario is exactly what happened. At the time and even now I wonder if her expectations got in the way of her family's progress and staying power. (Remember what Coyle said about the initial desire to play an instrument for a lifetime being the best predictor of success.) Or did this mother just know herself and her children well? All I can say is that every one of them was a delightful individual, each entirely different from the other. I loved working with all of them. For certain, this mother's clear-eyed candor remains unique in my forty-six years of teaching.

The opposite set of expectations came from a group of like-minded parents whose children once studied at Northwestern's then Division of Preparatory and Community Music. These parents and their children wanted to win competitions. This can be a laudable goal, but some caution is necessary. In his book *Flow: The Psychology of Optimal Experience*, Mihaly Csikszentmihalyi states, "Too much emphasis is placed on how children perform, and too little on what they experience. Parents who push their children to excel at an instrument are generally not interested in whether the children are actually enjoying the playing; they want the child to perform well enough to attract attention, to win prizes, and to end up on the stage of Carnegie Hall. By doing so, they succeed in perverting music into the opposite of what it was designed to be; they turn it into a source of psychic disorder."[3]

This particular group of parents moved their children en masse from teacher to teacher. Every fall they signed up with the teacher who had taught the first-place winner in the previous spring MTNA competition. Of course, the same teacher's student didn't win every year, so these children experienced nomadic study that was both fractured and chaotic.

We have all encountered the parent with the opposite expectation. I once took on two lovely children whose parents were so excited by their son's and daughter's first lessons that they dressed them up in fancy clothes and videotaped the whole affair. At the end of the lessons the dad said, "That was fantastic! I just hope every lesson they ever have will be this fun." Parents who say "fun" misguide their children into thinking playing the piano will be easy when it isn't. I told the parents that I, too, was happy everyone was so excited to study, but cautioned them. "I will do my best to keep the joy of music in your children's lives, but sometimes learning to play an instrument will be just plain hard work." They studied with me for only three years.

Then there is the intrusive parent. How do we handle them? One of my parents, an amateur jazz banjo player and drummer, came to his eleven-year-old son's lesson and announced: "Oliver will be playing 'Dizzy Fingers' at the spring recital," a different piece than his son and I had chosen. "It's impressive-sounding," he continued. He then began berating his son's performance of the piece.

When the father moved from the couch to the piano bench, still spouting his opinions, I stepped in front of him. "You hired me to be the teacher, Mr. X. Oliver and I will decide what he will play at the recital. The good news is, you can go relax and read. We have this situation in hand."

Surprisingly, the dad laughed. "You're right. I could use some downtime. I'm exhausted." He proceeded to stretch out on the couch and fall asleep!

On to the dissatisfied parent:

One summer morning the mother of one of our music camp's best string students came to me in a rage. This parent, the first-chair violist in a major symphony orchestra, wanted to let me know that the camp practice expectation of three hours a day was simply not enough for her twelve-year-old daughter. "She needs to practice at least five hours a day! The recreation and hiking program is preventing her from doing this. How will she ever make it in the music world?"

I listened quietly as she went on to say this same thing in several more ways. When she had calmed down a bit, I repeated what I had heard so she would know I understood what she had said, "So you think your daughter needs more practice time, and that the camp philosophy of mixing the physical activity of hiking with music study is getting in the way of this need."

The woman said, "Yes, you heard me correctly. I think you need to change this policy for everyone." I waited to see if she had more to say, but she seemed tapped out. Nevertheless, I asked, "Is there more?" "No," she said. "That's about it."

I thought awhile and then said, "Well, you are correct. The camp philosophy includes the mixture of serious practice and music-making with plenty of time to enjoy these glorious mountains around us by hiking in them. We feel these two activities combine to create a well-rounded musician." I wanted her to see if we agreed on what the camp philosophy was! "Yes, yes," she said, impatiently. "That's the problem."

"Well," I replied, "I understand what it is you want for your daughter, and you may be right. This may not be the camp for you. Maybe you would be wise to find another one that better fits what you are looking for."

The woman gasped. She stood there for at least a minute, speechless. Finally, she blurted out, "Oh no! We love it here! My daughter is having the time of her life. I am also enjoying it. We wouldn't think of leaving!"

"Good," I said, "I am happy to hear that, because we are enjoying you, too." I gave her a nod and walked away. The woman never had another complaint. She and her daughter attended the camp for several more summers.

THE FERTILE FIELD OF AFTER-SCHOOL CHILD CARE

In the late '80s Baldwin Piano and Organ Company and *Clavier* magazine joined together to produce three videoconferences for piano teachers in the United States and Canada. The brain child of the brilliant Tom Long, then director of music education at Baldwin, each of these live four-hour television productions reached over 11,000 piano teachers tuned in to satellite hookups at over forty locations in the United States and Canada. Long asked three usually separate music groups to join forces to make this event happen— colleges and universities, Baldwin piano dealers, and independent teachers' organizations. The result was an unprecedented series unsurpassed in its outreach even today, nearly thirty years later.

What was cutting-edge technology at the time seems quaint by today's standards. The live shows originated at Cincinnati's local PBS station, which provided the newsroom-like set and a bank of telephones behind the scenes. As moderator for all three shows, I joined each time with various highly regarded panel members, such as Nelita True, Martha Hilley, Larry Harms, Suzanne Guy, Marguerite Miller, and Ann Collins, to name a few. Panelists presented topics near and dear to teachers' hearts, but none was more pathbreaking than the one that discussed the business aspects of teaching. Participants at each of the satellite locations called in with questions, which

Tom Long copied onto cards and handed to me while we were on air; panelists answered each one depending on their varied expertise. Every show featured a survey. The most notable one asked teachers how much they charged per lesson, a fact that teachers prior to that time had kept close to their vests.

The excitement of these shows ignited a fire within teachers everywhere, and that included me. The challenge to go out and reach not only school-age students, but preschoolers, adults, and students who couldn't normally afford or have access to pianos and piano lessons sparked my desire to take my teaching into underserved locations. I quit my job as the Editor of *Clavier* magazine, and in 1988 I developed and instituted a program of piano lessons and supervised practice in the after-school child care programs in four Evanston, Illinois, public elementary schools.

This program reached many Title 20 students, who qualified for government help to pay for their child care. They neither had pianos at home nor many opportunities for traditional piano lessons, because of the cost and/or because they were in after-school child care. The superintendent of the Evanston District 65 Schools approved my plan as long as each school's principal agreed and as long as I charged students on a sliding scale so that everyone who wished to do so could participate.

Using three full-scale electronic keyboards provided by the Baldwin Piano and Organ Company plus the one upright located in each school, I set up my traveling studio in the schools' auditoriums. I hired three practice supervisors. Two were pedagogy students then studying at Northwestern University, and one was the mother of two of my former students. The program included a one-hour group lesson, which I taught at each school once a week, plus daily supervised group practice sessions lasting a half hour. I also supervised practice in one of the schools while my three assistants took charge of the other three.

The program immediately filled with students. Parents were happy to have lessons they could afford without the need to purchase a piano at home. Of course the day-care teachers loved us! We came to relieve them of six to eight of their charges every afternoon.

The three-to-a-group lessons, which I taught, were organized and orderly events that any teacher would recognize. What was revolutionary about the program was the supervised practice. Instead of sitting alone, playing five-finger tunes to the sound of their playmates happily running around outside, these children practiced with their peers, cheered on by practice supervisors, who had the advantage of being fresher than just-home-from-work moms or dads.

I originally envisioned the group practice as a quiet time for dutiful children to sit at their keyboards working on their carefully written-out assignments under the watchful eye of the supervisor. Yet when faced with the children's real-life, day-to-day leaning patterns, I quickly changed my expectations. The practice sessions soon evolved into less structured, even noisy times that included fifteen minutes of individual practice and fifteen minutes of musical games stressing cooperative learning.

The periods also called for a careful balance between form and freedom. I made daily, detailed practice outlines for each group, but counseled the three supervisors to feel free to adjust the plans to the children's passing moods, interest, and learning patterns. With the practice supervisors, I tried to devise practice routines that reflected the many ways group interaction stimulates learning.

In an article I published in Baldwin's winter 1990 *Soundboard*, I described a typical afternoon of practice.

Let's listen as I walk out to the playground, announce, "It's time for practice," and am greeted by the following:

Donald—Hey, Paul! It's keyboards time!

Colin—Please, Mrs. Kreader, let me practice with the second group. I'm busy on the slide.

Sheldon—Did you bring us Skittles?

Colin—What will you guys be doing today? Are we playing Musicopoly?

Paul—Can we make up songs?

Donald—Mine's gonna be about a mean robber, Paul. Wait 'til you hear it.

Colin—Okay, I'll come, but I only like to play songs with one line. Two lines are too hard. I'll only play "Sailing" and nothing else!

Joel—No, make Colin wait. Alex and I want to play "Heart and Soul." We want to go first.

Danielle—Can my friend Melissa come watch? She wants to hear me play.

Ryan—Good, you're here. I can go inside and get away from those boys. They're always bothering me.

Jeremy—Can we just get going and go?

This barrage of comments erupts all at once; I do little but stand there during the seeming confusion. Yet three main ingredients for learning are already present: excitement, interest, and most importantly, other children who share this enthusiasm. Even Colin, at first reluctant to give up his play to practice, feels the pull of the group and decides to join.

Confronted with a set of students, who has already spent a full school day sitting quietly, it is wise to find activities that allow for the children's pent-up physical and emotional energy. Once inside the room, the children divide into two groups. Those ready to settle down to individual practice choose one of the electronic keyboards and put on headphones. The others begin a musical game or project as far away from the keyboards as possible. The mood of the room encourages talking and helping but allows for children who wish to work in peace.

Noel—Mrs. Kreader, I don't remember where to put my fingers for "Mrs. Murphy's House."

Brad—I'll show him.

Noel—You think you know everything, Brad.

Brad—No, I don't.

Noel—I'll figure out where the fingers go myself—but, oh well, you can help me.

Jeremy—Could you guys be quiet?

Me—Try changing keyboards with Brad, Jeremy.

Children sometimes find learning frustrating. Yet if someone sits nearby ready to encourage them over the rough spots, they often find their own solutions to problems.

Jeremy—(Putting his head down on the keyboard) I hate this song!

Me—What do you hate about it, Jeremy?

Jeremy—I can't play the hands together at the end.

Ryan—Oh, yeah. Ick. I hated "Rockets," too, but see. I can play it now. Even fast. (Turns off the headphones and demonstrates out loud for Jeremy.

Jeremy—So?

Me—How did you learn to do that, Ryan?

Ryan—You told me to pretend like I was playing in slow-motion. But I had to play it a lot, a lot, a lot of times before I got it.

Colin—(Interrupting) Mrs. Kreader, Alex says this Musicopoly card says skip and I say it's a step. Who's right?

Me—Can you find the answer together? Where could you look?

Alex—Yeah, Colin. Let's look in our workbook.

Colin—(Returning to the game) Okay, but I know I'm right.

Jeremy—I have an idea! Just clap slowly, Ryan, and I'll play with you.

Colin—(At the game table) Okay, okay. So it was a skip. Big deal. Let's roll the dice.

When children solve their own problems, especially together, they begin to realize that learning occurs more rapidly when they are willing to make a few mistakes or to let someone help them. In addition, a non-judgmental attitude on the part of the supervisor creates an at-mosphere that allows for such mistakes and help. If I had told Colin his answer was wrong, which it was, he would have withdrawn from the group or, worse, created a disturbance. The neutral workbook answer not only kept the peace but gave the two boys a way to find future answers together.

A surge of progress often follows several days of seemingly un-focused and half-hearted work. Up-close observation of students' practice patterns supports this learning phenomenon. For three con-fused days, seven-year-old Jason's practice sessions include some ver-sion of the following conversation:

Me—Be careful, Jason. Which way do those notes tell you to go?

Jason—Higher.

Me—Are you certain?

Jason—They go to the right. That's higher.

Me—All the notes read from left to right, but some go higher toward the top of the page (shows arrow upward) and some go lower towards the bottom of the page (shows arrow downward).

Jason—I don't get it.

Several different explanations and games fail to relieve his mis-understanding. By the end of the week, Jason shuffles to practice, looking discouraged.

Jason—I just want to make up my own songs for today. I don't like this book.

Me—Okay. When you make up a piece you like, we will all come and listen to it.

For the next few sessions Jason uses his individual practice time to make up and perform his original improvisations to the delight of his classmates. An imaginative and humorous storyteller, Jason cracks everyone up. In the meantime, he continues to play group games that stress the difference between notes that go higher and notes that move lower.

A short time later, Jason greets me with a grin. "Now I get it." Pulling the neglected method book from his folder, he proceeds to sight-read seven new songs without a hitch. While few learning patterns display themselves as dramatically as Jason's, many children need extra time now and then to absorb certain concepts. Students who practice alone may be tempted to quit when the going gets rough. Group practice gives them the support of both the practice supervisor and fellow students and helps them weather the typical frustrations anyone faces when learning something new. Because I observe these patterns during practice periods, I can better structure the more formal once-a-week lessons.

The spring recital amazed all of us, me the teacher, the supervisors, parents, and yes, students. Every student came to the program as a beginner. Every student completed two levels of the method course. They played their recital pieces with confidence and without the usual stray notes here and there.

Children thought nothing of practicing every day; it was just something they did. In fact, a return to the pattern of one private lesson a week with practice at home was puzzling. Jeremy, who attended a different day care for the summer, came to my house for his first private lesson.

Jeremy—What time do I come tomorrow, Mrs. Kreader?

Me—Well, Jeremy, for the summer you will only see me once a week and you will practice at home.

Jeremy—That's weird. I don't like it.

Because someone was continually monitoring the children's practice, they quickly developed good reading habits and musicianship skills. By playing musical games together, they firmly cemented their understanding of note names, intervals, and other important concepts. In addition, no one played the wrong rhythm or pitches all week. I was freed from spending valuable lesson time reintroducing concepts and correcting mistakes and could present new material.

Parents, free of the taskmaster role, could simply enjoy their children's playing and progress. Best of all, every child of every economic background experienced the confidence and self-esteem that come with hard work and success.

Sheldon—Mrs. Kreader, how many pieces can we play for the recital?

Me—Choose your favorite three.

Sheldon—Three! I've got eleventy-hundred songs I could play. How can I choose just three?

The first year of the program, I stayed in the black. Depending on their family income, the students paid anywhere from $10 to $70 a month from September to June. I was able to pay the practice supervisors $10 an hour, which was fairly good pay in the late '80s. I, however, made only a few thousand dollars, not enough to keep up my end of the family finances. I began to look for outside funding, which I think I could have obtained, when a music publishing company approached me with a full-time job opportunity. While I couldn't turn this down, I left my year-long experiment and these special students with great reluctance.

The number of after-school programs in the United States has grown exponentially since the late '80s. "America After 3 PM," a research project published by Afterschool Alliance, reports:

> *Both the percentage and the total number of children in the United States participating in an afterschool program are on the rise. In 2014, 10.2 million children (18 percent) participated in an afterschool program, an increase from 2009 (8.4 million; 15 percent) and 2004 (6.5 million; 11 percent). Nearly one in four families (23 percent) currently has a child enrolled in an afterschool program.[1]*

The children are waiting.

THE REWARDS OF RISK

<hr>

Do you remember your first piano student? I certainly do. His name was Steve, and I was his fifth piano teacher in four years. It was 1974. I had just completed my master's degree in piano performance at Northwestern University. True, I had studied piano pedagogy with the legendary Fran Larimer, and had already taught several students as part of her practicum, but Steve was the first student I recruited on my own. His was the first warm body to enter The Barbara Kreader Piano Studio, as I called it in those days. (Marketing has come a long way.)

The pedagogy practicum students had been easy to teach. Most were beginners. Most were children of Northwestern faculty. In general they were intelligent, eager learners, whose parents encouraged them to practice. I taught no transfer students. I made lesson plans, followed the well-laid-out path of *The Music Tree*, and watched my little pianists grow.

My degree in hand, I left the safety of the pedagogy program and opened my own studio. With two young children and a husband who worked only part-time while he completed his doctorate, I needed financial stability as soon as possible. My sister-in-law designed a logo for me, and I put an ad in our local papers and the *Daily Northwestern*. This ad announced my recent degree and told prospective students that The Barbara Kreader Piano Studio featured three private lessons and one group lesson a month—a progressive approach to teaching at the time.

Several anxious weeks passed. The only person who called was a woman whose first question was: "What bus line runs by your studio?" My answer was the wrong one, so she hung up. After several more worried weeks, the telephone rang again. Bea Isaak, wife of then Northwestern piano faculty member, Donald Isaak, offered to take me to the local MTNA meeting. Bea, who was, and is, an inspired performer and teacher, introduced me to many of the veteran teachers in the area and helped me sign up with the group's teacher referral service.

Two days later the telephone rang. It was the prospective student's mother asking me if I had any openings. I assured her I did (I tried not to give away the fact that I had nothing but openings!) We made an appointment for an interview.

Steve, a fresh-faced, muscular boy of twelve, showed up in his ice-hockey uniform. Only the face mask was missing. His mother, a slightly anxious but charming woman, assured me her son was a musically talented boy, who loved the piano. He just couldn't find the right teacher. In four years his five teachers had not been able to teach him to read music.

Steve, who was several inches taller than I was, went to the piano. I asked him if he would play something for me, and he knocked out a credible rendition of the Chicago Blackhawks' theme song. That was it. Indeed, he couldn't read a note. Yet I immediately liked this boy. He had a goal. "I want to be the organist for a hockey team."

I needed Steve as a student as much as he needed me as a teacher, so I told his mother I would love to take him on. She was relieved that we could find a lesson time (I didn't show her my empty appointment book) and I described the once-a-month group lesson. (I had three weeks to find enough students to make up this group!)

The Music Tree, as excellent a method as it is, was not going to work with Steve. Even the adult version of that method didn't have music that Steve would like or understand. So I made my own appropriate method. I quickly learned that he had a good ear (at the time I couldn't play by ear myself) and that he loved jazz (I had absolutely no jazz experience).

I ran to my local music store (we had one then) and began a crash course in how to teach jazz. Thank goodness for John Mehegan. As the weeks progressed, Steve and I learned together. I began teaching him to read music with exercises away from the piano, and at the piano he picked out the melodies of several of his favorite songs. Eventually, Steve's reading and playing came together. The secret that unlocked the code was chords. Steve loved chords. I took a teaching tip from Frances Clark and taught them to him by feel and key-color using the Group I chords: C-G-F, Group II chords: D-A-E, and so on. After the first year he could play and name all of them at a breakneck speed, including all the variations of seventh chords.

The group lessons helped a lot. By that time I had three more students, but they were young beginners. Instead of mixing apples and oranges, I forced my own two children to join Steve's group. They were much younger than he was, but they liked Steve, who was a kind and funny companion. Both of my children became singer-songwriters rather than classical musicians. Maybe it all started then.

After two years Steve had a repertoire of eight or nine of the songs frequently heard at hockey games, including a more sophisticated version of the Blackhawks' theme. One day he literally ran up the stairs to his lesson. At the door he presented me with his card: "Steve LeMar, Organist for the Skokie Skatium." He had been hired to play during the adult and teen hockey league games at his local skating rink. He had reached his goal. After learning three or four more songs to round out his repertoire, Steve quit lessons. His music reading was still a struggle, but he could pick out melodies on his own and harmonize them. He played with fluidity and energy and yes, love.

Forty six years later I am able to choose which students I take. Sometimes I think this is a bad thing. Financial necessity caused me to take on a student who challenged me as a teacher in every way. Because of Steve, I learned how to play by ear, teach popular and jazz music, and teach someone who plays by ear how to read.

When the unusual student presents him or herself, take the leap. Together you will take an exciting musical journey. I am just as proud of Steve, who played at the Skatium all through high school, as I am of my student who is currently minoring in music at the University of Michigan. And remember, new teachers need your support. I am to this day in gratitude to the generosity of my friend Bea, who took me by the hand and helped me begin my life as an independent teacher.

THE MUSIC OF TEACHING

The eminent teacher Richard Chronister once wrote: "The importance of good technique, good reading ability, and good rhythm must never take precedence over the joy of music-making itself. Technique, reading, and rhythm are essential to successful music-making, of course, but the student's perception may be that we care more about a curved finger than we care about the music itself. I heard about a student's consternation when he heard his teacher say, 'Oh, isn't that a beautiful piece!' The student's wide-eyed response was, 'I didn't know you liked music!'"[1]

My student Matthew studied with me in the late '70s. Matthew's first recital was a formal event scheduled to take place in the daunting atmosphere of Northwestern University's Lutkin Hall. Matthew, then seven years old, couldn't have been more excited about performing his Bach minuet. We rehearsed the basics of recital etiquette—how to walk onto the stage, ways to adjust the bench, the best way to bow both before and after the performance.

The afternoon of the recital Matthew arrived wearing a navy-blue suit, white shirt, red tie, and new, white running shoes. His eyes sparkled with anticipation as he joined his fellow performers in the front-row seats. Each child before him took a turn trudging up the six steps to the stage, walking across its wide expanse, and playing his or her piece. When Matthew's turn arrived, he bolted from his seat, ran to the middle of the auditorium, and, forgoing the help of the steps, crawled up on the stage landing on his hands and knees immediately in front of the nine-foot Steinway. He got up, dusted himself off, and proceeded to play his minuet perfectly—despite an ankle-breaking tempo. When he bowed, the audience burst into laughter and loud applause. Matthew jumped off the stage and returned to his seat.

Every time I think of Matthew's eagerness to perform, of his joyful jump from the stage into the arms of the audience, this memory reignites my energy and enthusiasm for teaching.

Teaching is also a profession full of mysteries. These lyrics from the musical *The Fantasticks* speak volumes:

> *Plant a radish.*
> *Get a radish.*
> *Never any doubt.*
> *That's why I love vegetables;*
> *You know what you're about!*
> . . . .
> *While with children,*
> *It's bewilderin'.*
> *You don't know until the seed is nearly grown*
> *Just what you've sown.*[2]

Those of us who have taught for a long time often run into past students, some now grown up and nearly unrecognizable. Of course, we change, too. How many times have you run up to greet one of your former charges only to have them look at you blankly. The opposite also happens. A student hails you from afar, leaving you only seconds to remember his or her name.

Students can and often do surprise us. My former boss at Hal

Leonard Corporation, Herman Knoll, was an award-winning Indiana band director before entering the music publishing field. He often recounted the story of one of his students, a high-school boy who drove Herman crazy with his antics. At the time he was also not the most accomplished of band members. Herman was a tough taskmaster and he remembers being especially hard on this teenager. Years later, Herman, on a trip back to his Indiana hometown, heard a man call out his name from across the street. He eventually realized that the fellow approaching him was the grown-up version of this one-time difficult student. "Mr. Knoll, Mr. Knoll. It's so good to see you! You made such a difference in my life. Did you know I am now an award-winning band director just like you?"

Although we think we are teaching children how to be musicians who play the piano, sometimes we affect students in ways we know nothing about. The psychologist, author, and teacher Jack Kornfield tells the story of a high-school history teacher. One afternoon her students were especially inattentive and unruly. She stopped class, told them to close their textbooks, and asked them to get out a piece of paper. She went to the blackboard and wrote down the name of every student in the room. She asked the students to copy down the names. Beside each one she asked them to write a sentence or two that described why they liked or admired that person. At the end of the class she collected their lists.

A few months later, the class again teetered toward chaos. The teacher told the students she had something to give them—a list. Each student found his or her name at the top of the page. Following was the list the teacher had compiled of all the positive comments other students had written about them during the previous stormy day. The teacher did not comment or open a class discussion about the lists. She simply let the students read others' observations about them and dismissed the class.

Three years later, the high school teacher received the sad news that one of the young men in that class had been killed in the Persian Gulf War. At the man's funeral the teacher met up with his parents and three other former students.

> *The mother took out a worn piece of paper, obviously folded and refolded many times, and said, "This was one of the few things in Robert's pocket when the military retrieved his body." It was the paper on which the teacher had so carefully pasted the twenty-six things his classmates had admired.*
>
> *Seeing this, Robert's teacher's eyes filled with tears. As she dried her eyes another former student standing nearby opened her purse, pulled out her own carefully folded page and confessed that she always kept it with her. A third ex-student said that his page was framed and hanging in his kitchen; another told how the page had become part of her wedding vows.[3]*

As teachers we know not what we sow.

To quote the Trappist monk and author Thomas Merton: "The saints are what they are, not because their sanctity makes them admirable to others, but because the gift of sainthood makes it possible for them to admire everybody else."[4]

Teachers are what they are, not because their knowledge and expertise makes them admirable to students, parents, and other teachers, but because the gift of being a good teacher makes it possible for them to see and draw out the possibility in every student.

acknowledgments

This book took me forty-six years to write. It bears the influence of not only my teachers—Beth Miller Harrod, Laurence Davis, Fran Larimer, Don Schwartz, Paula Gorlitz, and Susan McConnell—but also of the many students who have taught me over the years.

To Jennifer Linn I send my gratitude for suggesting I write this book in the first place and for waiting five years for me finally to begin. I thank my poetry mentor, Alice George, for encouraging me to write it now!

Because much of the material in this book appeared in a different form in *Keyboard Companion* and *Clavier Companion*, I thank the late Richard Chronister and send much appreciation to Elvina Truman Pearce and Pete Jutras, whose fine editing skills sharpened and polished many of these essays.

I thank my *Hal Leonard Student Piano Library* co-authors, Fred Kern, Phillip Keveren, and Mona Rejino, for the wonderful work marriage that brought so much joy and new learning into my life. I am grateful to Keith Mardak and Herman Knoll, who gave me the opportunity to travel the world, meeting teachers and students not only from all over the United States but also from many different cultures. My gratitude goes to John Cerullo for believing in the book and to all the staff at Hal Leonard Performing Arts Publishing Group—

Lindsay Wagner, Godwin Chu, Wes Seeley, Cliff Mott, and Tilman Reitzle—for bringing it to publication.

I give grateful thanks to Linda-Marie Delloff, Gail Goepfert, Alice George, and Don Schwartz, who read my manuscript from vantage points outside of music. Your candid reactions improved and enlarged the original scope of the book. Without the support and encouragement of my fellow poets and Serious Players—Patrice Claeys, Catharine Jones, Betsy Merbetz, Marcia Pradzinski, Pat Price, and Catherine Ruffing—I might not have finished this project. To my Northwestern Rep Group friends of over thirty-five years—Marlene Chatain, Helen Grosshans, Bea Isaak, Barbara Kudirka, Edna TerMolen, and Rose Wood—thank you for sustaining me through the years.

I give special thanks to my children, Ben Kreader and Ellie Zwart, for the many childhood hours they spent listening to me teach, both at home and from the large closet in my studio at Northwestern. (It did have a nice lamp!) Keep singing your songs to the world.

Most of all, I thank my husband, Gregg, for sharing his stellar computer skills with me and for staying steady when I feared over and over again that I had sent the manuscript into the ethers with one wrong keystroke. I also thank him for bringing his cheerful warmth and Bugs Bunny wisdom into my life.

—BARBARA KREADER SKALINDER
NOVEMBER 14, 2015

notes

Introduction
  [1] Franklin, *It Itches*, x.

Enter the Portals to Piano Teaching's Past
  [1] Horwich, *Ding Dong School*, https:/archive.org/details/dingdongschool.

Students in a Virtual World
  [1] Adam is likely a member of Generation Z, the youngest generation. While definitions of generational starting points differ, Generation Z is most frequently defined as starting with those born in the early 2000s. The term "Net-Gener" is applied equally to Generation Y (also known as the Millennial Generation) and Generation Z. Tapscott, *Grown Up Digital*, 16.
  [2] Rideout, Foehr, and Roberst, Generation M2, 2.
  [3] Fleiss and Fisher, 21st-Century Intervention, 8.
  [4] Oblinger, *Boomers, Gen-Xers & Millennials*, 37–45. Prensky, *Digital natives, digital immigrants*. 5. Tapscott, *Grown Up Digital*.
  [5] Howe and Strauss, *Millennials Rising*, 55.
  [6] Carlson, *The Net Generation goes to college*.
  [7] Glenn, *Teaching the Net Generation*, 6–14.
  [8] Oblinger, Educating the net generation. Educause keynote.

The Pressured Child
  [1] Thompson and Barker, *The Pressured Child*, 19.
  [2] Thompson and Barker, *The Pressured Child*, 78.
  [3] Thompson and Barker, *The Pressured Child*, 78.
  [4] Coyle, *The Talent Code*, 112.
  [5] Thompson and Barker, *The Pressured Child*, xiv–xv.
  [6] Thompson and Barker, *The Pressured Child*, xv.
  [7] Chronister, *A Piano Teacher's Legacy*, 26.
  [8] Thompson and Barker, *The Pressured Child*, 59.
  [9] Thompson and Barker, *The Pressured Child*, 5.

The Twenty-First-Century Studio
[1] Anderson and Rainie, *The Future of Higher Education*.
[2] Anderson and Rainie, *The Future of Higher Education*.
[3] Anderson and Rainie, *The Future of Higher Education*.
[4] Anderson and Rainie, *The Future of Higher Education*.

Teaching to the Student and Not to the Test
[1] Chronister, *A Piano Teacher's Legacy*, 10.
[2] Chronister, *A Piano Teacher's Legacy*, 17.
[3] Chronister, *A Piano Teacher's Legacy*, 19.
[4] Chronister, *A Piano Teacher's Legacy*, 33.
[5] Chronister, *A Piano Teacher's Legacy*, 33.
[6] Chronister, *A Piano Teacher's Legacy*, 34.
[7] Chronister, *A Piano Teacher's Legacy*, 34.
[8] Chronister, *A Piano Teacher's Legacy*, 34.
[9] Chronister, *A Piano Teacher's Legacy*, 34.
[10] Chronister, *A Piano Teacher's Legacy*, 34.
[11] Chronister, *A Piano Teacher's Legacy*, 34.
[12] Chronister, *A Piano Teacher's Legacy*, 35.
[13] Kornfield, *Bringing Home the Dharma*, 48.

Let the Student Be Your Guide
[1] Chronister, *The Piano Teacher's Legacy*, 9.

Desire Equals Success
[1] Coyle, *The Talent Code*, 103.
[2] Coyle, *The Talent Code*, 104.
[3] Coyle, *The Talent Code*, 104.
[4] Coyle, *The Talent Code*, 101.

Some Struggle Is Not Only Necessary, It Is Valuable
[1] Coyle, *The Talent Code*, 74.
[2] Coyle, *The Talent Code*, 43.
[3] Coyle, *The Talent Code*, 51.
[4] Coyle, *The Talent Code*, 53.
[5] Csikszentmihalyi, *Flow*, 74.

Teaching Students How to Work on Their Own
[1] Lahey, *The Gift of Failure*, xxi.

Praise for Nothing Means Nothing
[1] Thompson and Barker, *The Pressured Child*, xiv.
[2] Thompson and Barker, *The Pressured Child*, 74.
[3] Lahey, *The Gift of Failure*, 21.
[4] Lahey, *The Gift of Failure*, 21.

Stickers, Skittles, and M&M's
[1] Lahey, *The Gift of Failure*, xix.
[2] Lahey, *The Gift of Failure*, 26.

NOTES

Perfectly Managing Imperfection
1. Westney, *The Perfect Wrong Note*, 61.
2. Coyle, *The Talent Code*, 43.
3. Westney, *The Perfect Wrong Note*, 61–62.

Failure: It's a Strength
1. Lahey, *The Gift of Failure*, xxi.
2. Lahey, *The Gift of Failure*, xxi.
3. Lahey, *The Gift of Failure*, xix.
4. Thompson and Barker, *The Pressured Child*, 50.
5. Lahey, *The Gift of Failure*, xx.
6. Lahey, *The Gift of Failure*, 34.
7. Lahey, *The Gift of Failure*, xxii.

Being Comfortable in Your Teacher Skin
1. Goldstein, *The Teacher Wars*, 5.
2. Goldstein, *The Teacher Wars*, 5.

Pay Yourself a Living Wage
1. Yost, *How I Made $100,000*, 17.
2. Yost, *How I Made $100,000*, 42.
3. Yost, *How I Made $100,000*, 43.

Parents as Partners
1. Lahey, *The Gift of Failure*, 184.
2. Lahey, *The Gift of Failure*, 185.
3. Csikszentmihalyi, *Flow*, 112.

The Fertile Field of After-School Child Care
1. Afterschool Alliance, *America After 3 PM*, www.afterschoolalliance.org/documents/AA3PM-2014/AA3PM_National_Report.pdf.

The Music of Teaching
1. Chronister, *Autumn Keyboard Companion, Editor's Notes.*
2. Schmidt, *The Fantasticks.*
3. Kornfield, *Jack Kornfield*, September 20, 2015.
4. Merton, *New Seeds of Contemplation*, 57.

bibliography

Alliance, Afterschool. *America After 3 PM.* 2014.

Anderson, Janna, and Lee Rainie. *The Future of Higher Education.* Pew Research Internet Project. 2012.

Carlson, S. "The Net Generation goes to college." *The Chronicle of Higher Education.* October 7, 2005. http://chronicle.com/free/v52/i07/07a03401.htm. (accessed December 5, 2012).

Chronister, Richard. *A Piano Teacher's Legacy.* Edited by E. Darling. New Jersey: The Frances Clark Center for Keyoard Pedagogy, Inc., 2005.

Chronister, Richard. "Autumn Editor's Notes." *Keyboard Companion,* 1991.

Coyle. *The Talent Code: Greatness Isn't Born. It's Grown. Here's How.* New York: Bantam Dell, 2009.

Csikszentmihalyi, Mihaly. *Flow: The Psychology of Optimal Experience.* New York: Harper & Row, 1990.

Fleiss, Alexandra, and Alexandra Fisher. *21st Century Intervention: Using Technology to Improve Student Academics and Behaviors.* 2014.

Glenn, J. M. "Teaching the Net Generation." *Business Education Forum* 54, no. 3 (2000): 6–14.

Goldstein, Dana. *The Teacher Wars: A History of America's Most Embattled Profession.* New York: Anchor Books, 2015.

Habit, Franklin. *It Itches: A Stash of Knitting Cartoons.* Loveland, Colorado: Interweave Books, 2008.

Horwich, Frances. *Ding Dong School.* Television. 1953.

Howe, N., and W. Strauss. *Millennials Rising: The Next Great Generation.* New York: Vintage Books, 2000.

Kornfield, Jack. *Bringing Home the Dharma.* Boston: Shambala Publications, Inc., 2011.

———. *Jack Kornfield.* September 20, 2015. jackkornfield.com (accessed November 14, 2015).

Lahey, Jessica. *The Gift of Failure: How the Best Parents Learn to Let Go So Their Children Can Succeed.* New York: HarperCollins, 2015.

Merton, Thomas. *New Seeds of Contemplation.* New York: New Directions Publishing Corporation, 1962.

Oblinger, D. 2004. http://www.educause.edu/e04/ conferencepresentationandresources/5269 (accessed June 2005).

Oblinger, D. "Boomers, Gen-Xers & Millennials: Understanding the New Students." *Educause Review*, 2003: 37–45.

Prensky, M. "Digital native, digital immigrants." *On the Horizon 9*, 2001.

Rideout, V. J., U. G. Foehr, and D. F. Roberst. *Generation M2: Media in the Lives of 8- to 18-Year-Olds.* 2012. www.kff.org/entmedia/8010.cfm. (accessed December 5, 2012).

Schmidt, Harvey and Tom Jones. *The Fantasticks.* New York. May 3, 1960.

Tapscott, D. *Grown Up Digital: How the Net Generation Is Changing Your World.* New York: McGraw Hill, 2009.

Thompson, Michael, and Teresa Barker. *The Pressured Child: Freeing Our Kids from Performance Overdrive and Helping Them Find Success in School and Life.* New York: Ballantine Books, 2005.

Westney, William. *The Perfect Wrong Note: Learning to Trust Your Musical Self.* New Jersey: Amadeus Press, LLC, 2003.

Yost, Kristin K. "How I Made $100,000 My First Year as a Piano Teacher." California: Kristin K. Yost, 2011.